ROCK 'N' ROLL'S STRANGEST MOMENTS

ROCK 'N' ROLL'S STRANGEST MOMENTS

Extraordinary tales from over fifty years
of rock music history

Mike Evans

ROBSON BOOKS

First published in Great Britain in 2006 by
Robson Books,
151 Freston Road
London
W10 6TH

An imprint of Anova Books Company Ltd

A CIP catalogue record for this book is available from the British Library

ISBN 1 86105 923 X

10 9 8 7 6 5 4 3 2 1

Typeset by SX Composing DTP, Rayleigh, Essex
Printed and bound by MPG Books Ltd, Bodmin, Cornwall

www.anovabooks.com

Contents

HOW MEAT LOAF GOT HIS NAME

DALLAS, TEXAS, *c.* 1947

There are a number of stories as to how Meat Loaf got his name, all relating to his days at school.

The most outrageous is that Marvin Aday (aka Meat Loaf) bet school friends that he would let them run a Volkswagen car over his head – which apparently they did, after which someone commented he must have been 'as dumb as a hunk of meat loaf'. Another version credits a football coach, who flung the hapless Aday off his team after the latter stepped on his foot, calling him a 'big hunk of meat loaf'.

Although he insists the story about the car running over his head is perfectly true, in his autobiography *To Hell and Back* Meat Loaf says he was dubbed with the nickname by his father from infancy – 'almost from the time my mother brought me home' – and it stuck with him through schooldays and adulthood.

Born Marvin Lee Aday on 27 September 1947 in Dallas, Texas, his mother was a preacher's daughter, a schoolteacher who sang in a local gospel quartet. His father by contrast was a big-built Dallas cop (who apparently knew Jack Ruby, the local hood who shot dead John F. Kennedy's assassin Lee Harvey Oswald) and an alcoholic, who not only tagged his offspring with the nickname but at one point attacked his teenage son with a knife. Small wonder, after his mother died of cancer, that Meat Loaf up and left for Los Angeles in 1967 where he embarked on a musical career, turning the derogatory nickname to his lifetime advantage.

THE ORIGINAL ROCK 'N' ROLL RECORD

MEMPHIS, 1951

Which was the very first rock 'n' roll record? It's a question that has long divided fans and critics, strong candidates being Bill Haley's 'Rock The Joint' from 1953 and Fats Domino's 'The Fat Man' (recorded in 1949); but, by general consent, rock 'n' roll's premiere platter was actually laid down in Memphis in 1951 by Jackie Brenston and his Delta Cats. Entitled 'Rocket 88', the series of incidents and accidents that led to its creation have become one of the genuine legends of early rock.

Jackie Brenston was born on 15 August 1930 in Clarksdale, Mississippi, a place name that reverberates through rock's prehistory. It was the birthplace of John Lee Hooker and where Muddy Waters made some of his earliest records; it is also where, legend has it, that bluesman Robert Johnson sold his soul to the devil at the crossroads of Highway 49 and Highway 61 one dark night back in the mid-thirties.

Returning to his home town after military service in 1947, Brenston got involved in the local music scene, both as a vocalist and booting saxophone player. He soon fell in with eighteen-year-old Isaiah 'Ike' Turner, a flashily dressed local DJ on station WROX, whose ambition extended far beyond the city limits of Clarksdale and who already had a band – the Kings of Rhythm – who had got together at high school. The band had just lost their lead singer, Johnny O'Neal, who'd split for the bright lights of Cincinnati and, although Ike sang himself, he was a vocalist short, and Brenston got the job, doubling on sax.

2

Blues guitarist B B King was the next to enter the picture. Still billed as 'Blues Boy', when he heard the Kings of Rhythm he told Ike they should be making some records, and promised to put them in touch with Sam Phillips in Memphis. Sam had just set up his Memphis Recording Service – the precursor to Sun Records where he would eventually pioneer rock 'n' roll with Elvis's first records – and was keen to get new rhythm and blues talent into the studio.

So, in March 1951, Ike Turner got the call from the man in Memphis. The Kings of Rhythm were ready to rock, and Ike's Chrysler was ready to roll, so the seven musicians crammed into the car with all their equipment and set off up Highway 61, thinking up new ideas for songs on the way.

In 1951, the fastest saloon on the road was reckoned to be the eight-cylinder Oldsmobile 88. Ads for the car featured a man and woman astride a space rocket, inviting motorists to 'ride the Rocket' – it sounded like something out of the R & B repertoire, where automobiles had long had a place as symbols of affluence and sexuality. So by the time the Kings of Rhythm were over the Mississippi/Tennessee state line and on the outskirts of Memphis, a song called 'Rocket 88' was just about finished for their recording debut.

The eighty-mile drive had been nothing if not eventful. Firstly, there was a flat tyre, the blow-out bringing them to a shuddering halt by the side of the road. The sight of a crowd of sharp-suited black men and a vehicle overloaded with musical instruments inevitably attracted the attention of the passing highway patrol, who hauled Ike off for questioning before letting them continue their journey. Then, back on the road, an amplifier belonging to guitarist Willie Kizart was loosely tied to the top of the car and slid off, bouncing down the highway behind them. Recovering the damaged amp, they continued their trek towards fame and fortune.

In the studio, the group cut four tracks with Phillips that day in March 1951, two featuring vocals by Ike Turner and two with Jackie Brenston singing lead. Brenston's numbers were 'Come Back Where You Belong' and their newly composed 'Rocket 88'. The latter track, with its honking saxophones and

Brenston's dynamic vocal, was like nothing Sam had heard before; plus there was a secret ingredient to the sound, achieved by accident when Sam stuffed the damaged amp's speaker cone with cardboard, giving a distorted guitar sound that was way ahead of its time.

Phillips, who was yet to set up his own label, leased the two singles from the session to Chess Records in Chicago; the Turner sides were billed as Ike Turner and his Kings of Rhythm while the Brenston single was credited as Jackie Brenston and his Delta Cats. Released in April 1951, by the end of the month 'Rocket 88' had made it into the national R & B charts, hitting the Number One spot in the June.

Despite the record's success, Jackie Brenston never followed through with another hit. He parted company with Turner, who was less than pleased about not being credited with the successful single, and Brenston's follow-up release 'My Real Gone Rocket' stalled at take-off. Ike Turner of course went on to bigger and better things, particularly in tandem with his wife Tina, and when Jackie Brenston rejoined the Kings of Rhythm late in the fifties as baritone sax player, Ike would let him sing the occasional vocal – but *never* 'Rocket 88'.

THE CRY GUY AHEAD OF HIS TIME

US, 1951

While not being a rock 'n' roll singer as such, Johnnie Ray was one of the pioneers of the link between a black R & B style and white pop singing that was subsequently forged solidly by Elvis Presley and others. And, more spectacularly, his emotional delivery and stage movements also pre-empted the Pelvis's gyrations that became a template for early rock 'n' roll.

Born in 1927, he had a minor US hit in 1951 with his first record 'Whiskey and Gin' after being helped on the way by R & B star LaVern Baker. Later that same year, 'Cry', backed with 'The Little White Cloud That Cried' took him to the top. The single was a huge hit, staying on the Number One spot in the American charts for eleven weeks, selling over a million copies and assuring Ray worldwide fame.

Four years before Elvis graced the charts and was being mobbed everywhere he appeared, Ray's equally emotive stage routine had teenage girls screaming, rushing the stage and literally trying to rip his clothes off. His tearful renditions of songs, where he would break down and cry as he sang, falling to one knee as he did so, not only predated Presley, but the stage and vocal dynamic of James Brown who emerged much later on in the decade.

Johnnie Ray's act, with its over-the-top histrionics, was easily caricatured of course, and he soon became the butt of stand-up comics and stage impressionists. The press had a field day whenever his concerts broke up in mayhem, which they often did, dubbing him variously 'the Cry Guy', 'the Nabob of Sob' and 'the Prince of Wails'.

As real rock 'n' roll took over in the mid-fifties, Johnnie Ray was seen as just another part of traditional and outmoded showbiz, and his later hits in the US tended to be energetic versions of corny oldies like 'Walking My Baby Back Home' and 'Alexander's Ragtime Band'.

He did, however, have a nearer-the-knuckle hit in the UK, with a cover of the Drifters' 'Such A Night' in 1954 which, although banned for its sexual suggestiveness by the BBC, made the top of the charts. And it was in the UK and elsewhere that Ray continued to be an attraction on the cabaret circuit, rather than in his native America, right up to his death from alcohol-induced liver problems in 1990.

Johnnie Ray, never really recognised in the history books of rock 'n' roll, holds a unique place nevertheless as a singer whose vocal manner – as much as Elvis's did half a decade later – shunned the music that had gone before, and became the very first stylist to address the new generation of teenagers.

THE RISE AND DEMISE OF MISTER ROCK 'N' ROLL

NEW YORK CITY, 1952–65

Flatbush Avenue in the New York borough of Brooklyn seems an unlikely address for one of the birthplaces of rock 'n' roll, along with more evocative locations like the Sun Studios in Memphis where the young Elvis cut his first sides, yet it was here – a full year before the hillbilly cat had his first nationwide hit with 'Heartbreak Hotel' and turned America and the rest of the world on its head – that a 33-year-old radio DJ from Cleveland hired the Paramount Theater and staged the first of a series of concerts that was to herald the rock revolution to come.

Alan Freed had started his nightly *Moondog Rock 'n' Roll Party* back in the Ohio city in 1952, spinning a potent playlist of black R & B records to an audience of predominantly white teenagers. This was radical stuff back in the days when pop meant Perry Como and Patti Page, and here was this guy with a gravelly voice – as often as not fuelled by a bottle of bourbon – playing Ruth Brown, Ivory Joe Hunter, LaVern Baker and other names which had up to then only meant something on 'race' record labels and in the black ghettos.

Freed's take on rhythm and blues was to dub it 'rock 'n' roll' – though he didn't actually invent the term – allowing him to bypass the latent prejudice against black-associated R & B, and soon he wasn't just plugging it on the airwaves, he started promoting it live.

A 'Moondog Coronation Ball' in March 1952 attracted 25,000 fans to a venue built for 10,000, and a near-riot ensued.

7

But what raised eyebrows across the state was the fact that more than half of the kids thronging to the gig were white. On the back of his burgeoning success in Cleveland, Freed relocated to New York in 1954, taking his nightly rock-ride to radio WINS. He repeated the live-show sensation at the Brooklyn Paramount in 1955, with a bill that included Fats Domino, the Drifters and Joe Turner. Again, the majority of kids that turned up were white.

Freed's finger was on the public pulse in more ways than one. He was one of the first, if not *the* first, to recognise that young people were now a powerful socio-economic group in their own right. Before the fifties, there were children and there were adults, and what came in-between was at best regarded as transitory, a temporary phase to be 'got over' as soon as possible, and at worst troublesome; even the word 'juvenile' was usually teamed with 'delinquent' in popular parlance. However, by this time America was waking up to the fact that here was a whole new bunch of people with money to spend. The media even invented a new word for them: 'teenagers'.

Over the next couple of years Freed was central to the rock 'n' roll explosion as it manifested itself in New York and across the nation, hustling deals for new artists, plugging obscure R & B acts with a conscious bias to music from the ghettos – he once famously boycotted Pat Boone's anodyne covers of black hits – and became as famous as many of the stars he helped find fame, appearing (as himself) in a number of rock 'n' roll exploitation movies including *Rock Around the Clock*, *Rock Rock Rock*, *Don't Knock the Rock* and a 1957 (very loose) biopic, *Mister Rock 'n' Roll*.

Freed also became a powerful force behind the scenes, thus receiving a number of dubious co-writing credits on songs he plugged, ensuring him half the composer royalty – though he did sometimes actually contribute to songs, most famously Chuck Berry's 'Maybelline'. However, trouble loomed in the latter half of the decade. In 1958, his television show *Rock 'n' Roll Dance Party* was cancelled when a camera showed doo-wop star Frankie Lymon dancing with a white girl, and later in the same year Freed was charged with incitement to riot when

8

trouble broke out at a concert he promoted in Boston. Though the charges were dropped seventeen months later, the legal fees from the case bankrupted him.

Then came the payola scandal. Prompted by allegations that certain contestants on TV quiz shows had been given the answers in advance to raise the excitement (and viewing figures); Congressional inquiries into broadcasting standards went on to investigate music programming, where the system of 'payola' – record-company pluggers paying to have a disc played – was widely practised. His name already tainted by the Boston affair and still disliked in many corners of the industry establishment for his bias towards black music, Freed was made the test case to Congress, a scapegoat for many others involved in backhanders in the industry.

He was subsequently fired from WABC radio in late 1959 for refusing to sign an affidavit denying he'd accepted payola, and this act of perhaps naïve honesty resulted in his being found guilty on 26 counts of commercial bribery in 1962. He got off with a fine and suspended sentence but the damage to his career was done. In 1964, unemployed and virtually an alcoholic, he was charged with income tax evasion. He died early in 1965, before the case came to trial.

In 1978 the movie *American Hot Wax*, with Tim McIntyre playing the renegade DJ, cast a more sympathetic light on Alan Freed's career than the rock 'n' roll industry he'd helped nurture ever did.

TRUCK DRIVER BLUES

MEMPHIS, 1953

The story of how the young Elvis Presley was signed up to Sun Records is a familiar one – the Memphis-based label providing a launching pad for his meteoric rise to fame – but lesser known are some of the let-downs Presley had before he ever got to cut a commercial record.

The day after he graduated from Humes High School in 1953, the eighteen-year-old started work at M B Parker Machinists' Shop for $33 a week. When Elvis famously stopped by the studios of Sam Phillips's Memphis Recording Service sometime that summer (ostensibly to make a personal 'walk-in' record costing $8 'to surprise his mother'), he was, in the words of Phillips' partner and receptionist Marion Keisker, 'shy, a little woebegone, cradling his battered, beat-up child's guitar'. While Elvis waited his turn to record a couple of tunes – 'My Happiness' and 'That's When Your Heartaches Begin' – he asked Miss Keisker if she knew of any groups looking for a singer, but she replied that she didn't.

Over the next few months, Elvis hung around the studio and its office – he knew he wanted to be a singer, but had no idea of how to go about becoming one. He started to dress like the sharp black rhythm and blues performers who hung out around downtown Beale Street, and grew his hair with a raffish quiff and sideburns. In fact the long hair was his reason for leaving the machinists' shop (his boss wanted him to get it cut) and take a job driving a truck for Crown Electric at $40 a week in April 1954.

Then, just a month later, Elvis thought his time had come. A friend called Ronnie Smith, who Elvis had played the odd gig with, was now playing in a real group, a full-time professional outfit led by Eddie Bond. Bond was something of a veteran on the local scene, having played since he was fifteen and now getting back into the local venues after a period in the navy. Elvis bumped into Ronnie one day, who told him that Bond was looking for a singer for the band, and suggested he try for the job.

The young hopeful turned up at the Hi Hat club where Eddie Bond was rehearsing and ran through a couple of songs with the band, but Bond wasn't impressed. In retrospect, Bond claimed it was the club's owners who didn't like Presley but, for whatever reason, he turned him down – apparently caustically telling him to stick to driving a truck, 'because you're never going to make it as a singer'.

A few months later and Elvis Presley had recorded 'That's All Right (Mama)' for Sun Records. After the disc started to make a big impression in Memphis and then across the South, Eddie Bond had Ronnie Smith ask Elvis if he'd like to sing with them now. The ex-truck-driver, polite as was always his way, said thanks, but no.

GUITAR SLIM, FIRST SHOWMAN OF RHYTHM AND BLUES

NEW ORLEANS, 1954

The use of outlandish theatrics in a performance has been around a long time in rock 'n' roll, and in the rhythm and blues that preceded it – some of the earliest reported examples were displayed back in the blues days by Charley Patton in the juke joints of the Mississippi Delta during the twenties. Patton was known for his lively stage presence, dancing around while he played the guitar between his legs or behind his back. Numerous other blues and R & B artists adopted some form of a stage act throughout the years. Howlin' Wolf had his tail-dragging routine, the onstage banter of Louis Jordan and his band made them a top draw in the forties, and showmanship certainly came to the forefront in the guise of Jimi Hendrix and Buddy Guy as they roared across the large festival and stadium stages in the sixties and seventies. However, without question, the unsurpassed master of over-the-top presentation was Guitar Slim, who was one of the architects of rock 'n' roll style and a sensation around the clubs of New Orleans during the fifties.

Guitar Slim was born Eddie Jones in Greenwood, Mississippi in 1926. When he was five years old his mother died and, having never known his father, he was sent to Hollandale to be raised by his grandmother on the L C Haves plantation. There he learned to make a living working in the cotton fields and ploughing behind a mule.

As a kid, Eddie would spend his free time at the local juke joints in Hollandale and very soon he was sitting in with the bands as a singer and dancer – his adept skills as a dancer earning him the nickname 'Limber Legs'.

While still in his early teens he took up the guitar, influenced in particular by the Delta slide-guitar legend, Robert Nighthawk, and Texas players T-Bone Walker and Clarence 'Gatemouth' Brown. In fact it would be Gatemouth's 'Boogie Rambler' that Jones would use as his theme song for several years.

By 1950, he had relocated to New Orleans, where he began to develop a new guitar sound, experimenting with distorted overtones, feedback and such a decade and a half before Jimi Hendrix. This brought him to the attention of the Imperial label in 1951, for which he cut four songs, all to prove less than successful. Next he tried the Nashville-based Bullet label in 1952 and enjoyed a modest regional hit with the single 'Feeling Sad'; but although this in turn attracted the prestigious Specialty Records where he would have his biggest success, it was his totally unique live appearances that attracted as much attention as his records with audiences.

Having now renamed himself 'Guitar Slim', Jones developed a stage act that none could forget. He would wear specially tailored, garishly coloured zoot suits, with shoes and bizarrely dyed hair to match. An assistant would follow him during his shows, carrying up to 350 feet of guitar cord plugged into an amp (usually adjusted to a deafening volume), not missing a note if Slim decided to walk through the audience. On occasion, Slim would ride on the assistant's shoulders, while his big gimmick was to walk through the audience to the back of the venue, out of the entrance of the club and into the street – still playing his solid-bodied guitar at top volume. It was not unusual for him to bring traffic to a halt! Through all this, of course, his audiences would go berserk.

The key to his success at Specialty was the 1954 single 'The Things That I Used To Do', which was produced by the New Orleans legend Cosimo Matassa and featured Lloyd Lambert's band backing him up with special guest Ray Charles filling in on the piano. Slim would claim the song came to him in a dream, where a devil and angel fought each other with their own sets of lyrics. Of course, being a raunchy R & B number, the devil's lyrics had won out. Regardless of what inspired it, the song rode the R & B charts for 21 weeks, six of them at Number One, and would sell over a million copies.

But success was marred by Slim's hard drinking and womanising lifestyle. He was said to be drinking 'a pint of gin and chasing it with a fifth of black port every day', a recipe for disaster. Early in 1959, the band set out for an East Coast tour despite the breathing problems Slim was having as a result of his alcoholism. On 6 February, the band were in Rochester, New York, when Slim became violently ill. He was told by a local doctor that he needed to give up drinking and the next day in New York City the band had to carry an incapacitated Slim to his hotel room. At the time, they believed he was just drunk but later, when they couldn't revive him, a doctor was called. But it was too late – Guitar Slim had died of bronchial pneumonia, a condition worsened by his drinking. He was just 32 years old, and was buried in an unmarked grave with his guitar.

At the time, his death was overshadowed by the plane crash that had taken the lives of Buddy Holly, Richie Valens and The Big Bopper only four days earlier, but in retrospect Guitar Slim deserves a place in the history books as one of the original showmen of the electric guitar and a model for scores of rock 'n' roll players to come.

HOW ROCK'S FIRST ANTHEM ALMOST DIDN'T HAPPEN

NEW YORK CITY, 1954

It would be the third biggest-selling single of all time, yet 'Rock Around The Clock' by Bill Haley and His Comets nearly didn't get made at all, and even when it did was initially released as the B-side of a single.

'Rock The Joint' and 'Crazy Man Crazy' had been minor hits for Haley and the band in 1952 and 1953 respectively; in fact, 'Rock The Joint' was credited with inspiring DJ Alan Freed to coin the phrase 'rock 'n' roll' to describe this new take on black R & B. On the strength of that, they were offered 'Rock Around The Clock' (originally recorded by Sonny Dae), a lightweight number in the same vein written by James Myers (aka Jimmy De Knight) and Max Freedman. However, Jimmy Miller, the boss at their record company Essex, didn't like it and Haley tried three times to record the song, only to have Miller tear up the sheet music there and then in the studio. The solution came when they moved from Essex to the Decca label in 1954.

The date for the session was set for 12 April 1954, and the studio for what became a legendary recording was a former ballroom in Manhattan called the Pythian Temple. Decca had been using this huge auditorium-like hall for years. Its cavernous high ceiling and great walnut-panelled walls created a natural reverberation chamber, which added a unique strength and volume to any music played there. Producer Milt Gabler had recorded some of his best work here in what Decca called their Studio A, which was now fitted out with new 'state-of-the-art' high-fidelity recording equipment.

The band very nearly didn't make it to the recording studio. En route to New York for the session, a ferry they were travelling on was grounded in the middle of the Delaware River, holding up the session for most of the day – and apparently leaving Sammy Davis Jr waiting in the lounge for a session he'd been booked into. And when the group did get there, Milt Gabler decided they should record a number he'd written first, 'Thirteen Women (And Only One Man in Town)'. The song, with its bizarre theme about the only survivors of an H-bomb blast being one man and thirteen women, took Haley and the boys six takes to get right, leaving them only forty minutes for 'Rock Around The Clock'.

It was 'Thirteen Women' that was picked as the A-side of the single, being in the style of the jump-band novelty numbers of Louis Jordan that had had a proven audience. Released on 15 May, it did reasonably well, selling over 75,000 copies, but 'Rock Around The Clock' composer Myers wasn't satisfied and he sent copies of Bill Haley's B-side song to every producer in Hollywood.

Bill Haley and His Comets, meanwhile, were forging ahead. They had a huge R & B hit that same year with a cover of Joe Turner's 'Shake Rattle And Roll', followed by a Top Twenty entry with 'Dim Dim The Lights'. Who needed 'Rock Around The Clock'?

Then came a non-musical black-and-white movie about juvenile delinquency in schools entitled *Blackboard Jungle* in which the director decided to play 'Rock Around The Clock' over the credits. Apparently it was Peter Ford, the son of the film's lead actor Glenn Ford, who suggested the number to director Richard Brooks. *Blackboard Jungle* hit movie screens in March 1955. By 5 July, the day before Bill Haley's thirtieth birthday, Haley had a huge hit on his hands. Teenagers rioted in cinemas whenever the tune was played, and Decca had fortuitously re-released the single, this time with '. . . Clock' as the A-side. It hit the top of the charts on both sides of the Atlantic, catapulting Bill Haley to superstardom, and triggering the worldwide rock 'n' roll revolution nearly a year before Elvis had his first chart entry.

The record remained high profile when it lent its name (and music) to what is considered the first full-length rock 'n' roll movie, 1956's *Rock Around the Clock,* which also provided Haley with his acting debut. It re-entered the charts and has eventually clocked up sales figures of nearly 30 million over the years since. Not bad for a record that nearly didn't get made at all.

CASH SPINS ELVIS DISCS

TEXAS, 1955

In the early days of the pioneering Sun Records label in Memphis, there was a certain amount of natural rivalry between the new clutch of rockabilly artists that producer and label owner Sam Phillips was nurturing to stardom. One of the names signed up at the time was the then-unknown Johnny Cash, who with guitarist Luther Perkins (brother of another Sun star Carl Perkins) and bassist Marshall Grant released his first sides as part of the Tennessee Three. His debut disc on the label was released in 1955, 'Cry, Cry, Cry' backed with 'Hey Porter'.

Although the trio continued to pump out such hits as 'I Walk The Line', 'Get Rhythm' and 'Folsom Prison Blues', Cash got increasingly frustrated by the fact that Phillips was spending more and more of his time, energy and money promoting the career of the young Elvis Presley, whom he saw as the potential jewel in the label's crown.

Cash and the boys were heading out for some gigs in Texas on one particular occasion when Phillips asked them a favour. It seems Elvis was riding high in the local charts around the South with one of his Sun singles, and Sam told Cash he needed to get some copies of the record over to Texas. He'd fill the boot of their car with the discs, so they could give them to the promoter they were working for when they arrived.

Crossing over a high ridge as they headed southwest, Johnny couldn't resist the temptation to stop the car and sail one of the discs off the edge of the cliff. Of course, this looked too much like fun, so soon the entire stock of Presley platters was flying through the air into the canyon below, never to make it to their destination in the Lone Star state.

THE DEATH OF JOHNNY ACE

HOUSTON, TEXAS, 1955

The marvellously named Johnny Ace is remembered for two things: a fine single called 'Pledging My Love' that made Number One in the American R & B charts in February 1955 before entering the national pop Top Twenty; and the fact that his was the first 'rock 'n' roll suicide'.

Suicide is, perhaps, not strictly accurate, though Ace's death was clearly self-inflicted, and not entirely accidental. On the other hand, the laws of chance, or the 'fickle finger of fate' that has been blamed for so much over the years, certainly played a part in his demise. Johnny Ace, at the age of just 25, blew his own brains out in a bizarre backstage game of Russian roulette.

Johnny, whose real name was John Marshall Alexander Jr, was born in Memphis in 1929; by the time he was twenty, he was playing piano with the seminal Memphis outfit the Beale Street Blues Boys. The Blues Boys included vocalist Robert Calvin Bland, later famous as Bobby 'Blue' Bland, and guitarist Riley 'B B' (for Blues Boy) King.

When B B left to go solo in 1952, Bland was drafted into the army, so Johnny took the latter's place as lead singer. And so it was that Johnny Ace (his name changed to protect the reputation of his preacherman father, the Reverend John Alexander) began releasing records from mid-1952 as featured vocalist with a reshuffled line-up now billed as the Beale Streeters.

He'd signed with the newly formed Duke label, and his first release 'My Song' shot to the top of the R & B chart. Ace's fine baritone voice rendered him four more R & B charters under his belt by the end of 1954, which were usually smooth ballad topsides with a bluesy rocker on the flip, and he'd also become a star name on the southern rhythm and blues circuit.

It was Christmas Eve 1954, and he was sharing the bill at the City Auditorium in Houston, Texas with Willie Mae 'Big Mama' Thornton (who was enjoying a hit in the R & B bestseller list with the original 'Hound Dog'). Ace had just recorded his next single 'Pledging My Love', which was to be released in early January 1955.

Johnny was backstage, fooling around with his .32 revolver. This was nothing new – those around him were used to him brandishing a loaded pistol in hotels, dressing rooms and such. He'd often play a solo version of Russian roulette – spinning the chamber and clicking the trigger with a one-in-six chance of the hammer landing on the single live bullet as he held the gun to his temple. But this was the night his number came up, as Johnny pulled the trigger and half his brains ended up on the other side of the room.

'Pledging My Love' was released as planned in January 1955; by February it topped the R & B list and made Johnny Ace's only entry into the national *Billboard* Top Twenty.

The posthumous success of 'Pledging . . .' and the newsworthy circumstances of Johnny's death were a double bonus as far as the record industry was concerned. Just a week after the single was released, and less than three since Johnny wielded his weapon for the last time, the first tribute record appeared – Valetta Dallard singing 'Johnny has Gone'.

Next came a double-sided dedication, 'Why Johnny Why' by Johnny Moore, backed with 'Johnny Ace's Last Letter' by Frankie Irwin. More were to follow, plus a couple of posthumous releases by Johnny Ace himself. In total, his death had triggered (no pun intended) just as many releases as the silver-voiced singer was responsible for during his short lifetime.

THE STRANGE STORY OF 'LOUIE LOUIE'

US, 1955–65

It's rare that a song takes on a life of its own, but that certainly was the case of 'Louie Louie', one of the most celebrated – and for a time notorious – tunes in the history of rock 'n' roll.

The original 'Louie Louie' was written in 1955 by Richard Berry and in 1957 was recorded with the Pharaohs and released as a single on Flip Records. Richard – a respected member of the local Los Angeles doo-wop music community – created a catchy, calypso-type number that was originally intended as the B-side for his recording of 'You Are My Sunshine'. Although Berry's version was a moderate success in the Los Angeles area, he wound up selling the publishing rights when he felt the song had run its course. Yet somehow, instead of fading into obscurity, 'Louie Louie' was adopted by various American bar bands and became especially popular in the Pacific Northwest region.

As the legend goes, up in Tacoma, Washington, Rockin' Robin Roberts, a singer with a group called the Wailers, picked up on Richard Berry's catchy little single, and decided to cover the song in a completely new style. Playing around with the song, the Wailers added their own variations, with Rockin' Robin belting out the words like an inspired gospel chant and Rich Dangel adding what became a legendary guitar solo, releasing what was the first rock 'n' roll version of the song. Released on the band's own Etiquette Records, the song became a regional hit in the Seattle–Tacoma area.

Although the single never made an impression nationally, the Wailers had a solid following in the northwestern states of Washington and Oregon, and the popularity of the actual song went from strength to strength. Other bands had been playing it ever since the Richard Berry original had appeared, and by the early sixties it had become something of a regional anthem in the Northwest.

Next into the picture came two local bands based in Portland, Oregon: the Kingsmen and Paul Revere and the Raiders. Both bands caught the 'Louie Louie' bug, and decided to record it themselves, and both recorded the song at Bob Lindahl's recording studio within a week of each other in April 1963.

The Kingsmen initially recorded the song as a demo for a gigging job on a cruise liner, and apparently hated the result, not even wanting it released. Lead singer Jack Ely, so the story goes, had to sing his version of Berry's almost-incoherent patois lyrics into a microphone suspended near a fifteen-foot ceiling. And they were even more disenchanted when they discovered they had to pay the $50 recording fee! Locally it came a poor second to the Paul Revere version, which made the major impact across the Northwest area. Yet six months later the song was known across the nation, with the Kingsmen's version climbing to the Number Two position in the US charts.

The reason for the unexpected success – indeed notoriety – of the song lay in the lyrics, which in truth were hardly decipherable. Lines like 'Tell her I'll never leave her again' were being interpreted by over-prurient listeners as 'Tell her I'll never lay her again', leading to the conclusion that the lyrics were disguising various obscenities. Reflecting the views of 'concerned parents', the record was actually banned in Indiana, the governor's press secretary stating that the words were 'indistinct but plain if you listen carefully'.

And things didn't stop there. The National Association of Broadcasters, the US Department of Justice and the Federal Communications Committee all launched investigations into the lyrics of 'Louie Louie', with FBI agents trying to locate Richard Berry to see what he meant by such lines as 'A fine little girl, she wait for me / Me catch the ship across the sea.' At one stage FBI men were slowing down the 45-rpm disc to 33⅓ in order to unearth any hidden obscenities. After an incredible two years of investigation and a 120-page report, the authorities finally ruled that the song was not pornographic, and the obscene interpretations put on it by 'concerned' citizens were 'imagined filth'.

The song thereby took its place in the rock 'n' roll hall of fame as one of the most celebrated ever, and was covered by a huge array of artists. There have been over 1,600 versions of 'Louie Louie' released on record, among the most familiar names covering it including – as well as Paul Revere & the Raiders and the Kingsmen of course – Mongo Santamaria, the Kinks, Stanley Clarke & George Duke, Ike & Tina Turner, Otis Redding, Barry White, the Flamin' Groovies, Motorhead and a sexiest-of-all version by smoky-voiced diva Julie London.

HOW A DO-IT-YOURSELF JAZZ CRAZE CHANGED ROCK

UK, 1956–7

The British jazz scene in the first half of the fifties was very strictly divided into two camps of followers. There were the modernists, who favoured all that had developed in jazz since the big-band era of the thirties and forties, the explosion of bebop and all the 'modern jazz' that followed it. In addition, there were the traditionalists, who spearheaded a revival in the 'original' jazz of New Orleans and Chicago that had preceded the big swing bands, including legendary players from the twenties like King Oliver, Jelly Roll Morton and the young Louis Armstrong.

One thing both camps had in common, however, was that they despised rock 'n' roll as commercialised rubbish, played and sung by incompetents! Few in the UK jazz community recognised rock music's roots in urban rhythm and blues, or the country blues that came before. Indeed, urban R & B from America was a virtually unknown quantity, and earlier 'pure' blues was largely considered a part of folk music.

However, it was the purist jazz world of the early fifties that produced one of the most unlikely building blocks of the British rock scene of the sixties – the do-it-yourself phenomenon known as skiffle.

One of the crucial bands of the 'trad' movement, as the revivalist trend became known, was Ken Colyer's Jazzmen; but trumpeter Colyer was a bona fide purist, and when he decided to travel to New Orleans to hear what was left of the 'real thing',

25

the rest of the band continued with a new trumpet player under the titular leadership of trombonist Chris Barber.

The line-up of the Chris Barber Jazz Band, which by 1954 was one of the biggest names in the growing trad-jazz craze, included a banjo player in the rhythm section by the name of Lonnie Donegan. Born Anthony Donegan in 1931, he'd adopted the name Lonnie from one of his heroes, the American blues singer Lonnie Johnson, and would sing occasional blues and gospel-oriented numbers with the band. This proved popular with fans, as did a 'band within a band' that featured Donegan on guitar, singing blues, African-American work songs and such, as a folky interval to the mainly instrumental band set.

They called the interval line-up their 'skiffle group', skiffle being a term used to describe twenties 'jug band' music played with guitars and various improvised 'home-made' instruments such as jugs, washboards and kazoos. Early in 1955, two tracks recorded for the 1954 Barber album *New Orleans Joys* were released as a single under the banner of the Lonnie Donegan Skiffle Group.

The single, on the UK Decca label, consisted of 'Rock Island Line' backed with 'John Henry'; numbers originally recorded by folk-blues singer Huddie 'Leadbelly' Ledbetter. With a long spoken introduction by Donegan, the top side – with Lonnie on guitar, Barber on bass and Beryl Bryden on washboard – stunned the whole music world when it made the Top Ten in both Britain and America (an unheard-of feat in those days), selling over a million copies.

The American success of 'Rock Island Line' was a one-off, but in the UK it triggered a string of hits for Donegan of totally unexpected proportions. He was offered a US tour on the back of his first hit, for which he was obliged to leave Barber and form his own permanent skiffle group. And although he didn't follow up his success in America, between 1956 and 1959 he had no less than twenty entries in the UK Top Twenty, including chart-toppers 'Cumberland Gap' and 'Gamblin' Man', both in 1957.

Donegan's repertoire drew on American folk music,

26

particularly the songs of Leadbelly and Woody Guthrie (half a decade before Bob Dylan cast a spotlight on the folk legend), and was an unlikely bedfellow with burgeoning rock 'n' roll in the nation's pop charts. However, in the wake of Lonnie's success, scores of skifflers made records, with a few memorably charting. These included Chas McDevitt's 'Freight Train' and the Vipers Skiffle Group with two Donegan covers ('Don't You Rock Me Daddy-O' and 'Cumberland Gap'), all in 1957. But apart from Lonnie Donegan, who had UK Top Twenty hits through into the early sixties, the skiffle boom was short-lived as far as the charts were concerned.

The true impact of skiffle, however, was manifest in thousands of youthful groups springing up all over the British Isles – do-it-yourself outfits with a washboard and tea-chest-bass 'rhythm section' fronted by one or two highly enthusiastic budding guitarists. The very nature of the repertoire – simple 'authentic' songs about railroad men, escaped convicts and such – was a million miles from rock 'n' roll per se, but lent itself ideally to the amateur skiffler's untutored approach.

This resulted in a veritable army of would-be guitar players who would musically come of age in the early sixties. These included some of British rock's leading lights like Eric Clapton, Jimmy Page, Jeff Beck and many more. And the British beat and R & B groups that revolutionised rock in the sixties almost all started as skiffle outfits: the Beatles (as the Quarrymen), the Rolling Stones, Kinks, Animals and many more all had their roots in the skiffle boom.

Alongside the rise of rock 'n' roll in the late fifties, when Elvis, Little Richard, Buddy Holly and the rest transformed popular music forever, it was the parallel boom in home-grown skiffle that literally put guitars into the hands of a generation of musicians who would change things just as radically through the following decade.

THE FIRST 'ROCK 'N' ROLL' HITS

US/UK, 1956

The first record with 'rock 'n' roll' in the title to make the charts in both the United States and Great Britain, was in fact not a rock 'n' roll record at all. It was an early cash-in on the new craze by ex-Glenn Miller vocalist Kay Starr. Released in January 1956, 'Rock and Roll Waltz' topped the charts on both sides of the Atlantic.

Meanwhile, the first British-made record to have 'rock 'n' roll' in its name was from an even more unlikely source. It was not Tommy Steele (although he *did* follow with 'Rock with the Cavemen' a month later), Cliff Richard or any other early Brit beatster – but was by the surreal radio comedy team of the Goons, consisting of Peter Sellers, Spike Milligan and Harry Secombe. Entitled 'Bloodnok's Rock 'n' Roll Call', it was one side of a two-sided hit that got to Number Three in the UK Top Ten in September 1956, with 'The Ying Tong Song' on the flip.

THE RHYTHM ORCHIDS' CHART DOUBLE-UP

CLOVIS, NEW MEXICO, 1956

The Rhythm Orchids were one of the original rockabilly acts in rock 'n' roll, and responsible for one of the most unusual releases in chart history – a single which was a two-sided hit under two different artist credits, then released as two separate singles to make the best-sellers all over again.

The group was fronted by singer–guitarist Buddy Knox who was born Buddy Wayne Knox in 1933 in Happy, Texas. In 1948, aged fifteen, he wrote a song called 'Party Doll', which became part of the repertoire when he later formed a group, The Rhythm Orchids, in 1955. Knox was a student at West Texas University at the time, and the outfit featured himself on guitar and vocals, Jimmy Bowen on bass, and Don Lanier on lead guitar; Dave Alldred was subsequently added on drums. As did many other groups recording in West Texas in the fifties, Buddy's group eventually found their way to Norman Petty's studio in Clovis, New Mexico, the same studio where Buddy Holly and the Crickets started their recording career.

When the group went into the studio, a unique sound emerged due to the fact that producer Petty did not really know at the time how to record rock 'n' roll drums, so he used a cardboard box instead of a drum kit. In 1956, the group recorded Knox's old composition 'Party Doll', crediting it to Buddy Knox with the Rhythm Orchids; at the same session they recorded 'I'm Stickin' With You' with bass player Jimmy Bowen on vocal, credited as Jimmy Bowen with the Rhythm Orchids.

The enterprising Knox then formed his own record label, naming it Triple-D after the KDDD radio station in Dumas, Texas. The two songs were issued as both sides of a 45 single on the Triple-D label, and began to gain in popularity as they received local airplay – suddenly the Rhythm Orchids had a two-sided hit on their hands.

But things really took off when the newly formed Roulette label in New York City picked up both songs in 1957 and decided to release each separately with a different B-side. The result was a million seller for each song, with 'I'm Stickin' With You' by Jimmy Bowen getting to Number Fourteen in the *Billboard* chart, while 'Party Doll' went all the way to the Number One spot.

Through 1957 and 1958, Buddy Knox and the Rhythm Orchids placed a total of eight songs in the charts which they had recorded on the Roulette label, including 'Rock Your Little Baby To Sleep', 'Hula Love' (which made the Top Ten) and 'Somebody Touched Me'.

Jimmy Bowen managed to put four songs in the Top 100 before becoming a top record executive and producer on the West Coast. He worked for the Chancellor and Reprise labels before moving to MCA Records in Nashville in the seventies. The giant MCA company was renamed Universal Records in 1988, with Bowen as its president.

Buddy Knox, meanwhile, moved into mainstream pop and had a solo hit with his own song, 'Lovey Dovey', in 1961. He later moved on to country music, where he had a minor hit with 'Gypsy Man' (aka 'Gipsy Man') in 1968. He moved to Canada and in the early seventies opened a nightclub in Vancouver called the Purple Steer. Later diagnosed with cancer, he passed away on 14 February 1999.

THE MISSING QUEEN OF ROCK 'N' ROLL

HOLLYWOOD, 1956

If it had not been such a male preserve in its early days, a pretty black-haired singer by the name of Wanda Jackson could have easily been hailed as the First Lady of rock 'n' roll – a female Elvis no less.

Born in Oklahoma in 1937, Wanda Jackson was still in high school when country singer Hank Thompson heard her sing on an Oklahoma City radio show and asked her to record with his band. She started doing gigs around the Southwest and in 1955 met Elvis Presley while he was still with Sun Records, when she played support on one of his local tours. Still doing country-style ballads and gospel songs, it was Presley (whom she dated a few times) that encouraged the youngster to try her hand at rock 'n' roll – 'Elvis talked me into doing the rock thing,' she would later recall.

She developed a wild style of rockabilly that got her signed to Capitol Records in Hollywood a year later, who felt she could be the female answer to their star rocker Gene Vincent. Wanda Jackson made some amazing records, including 'Hot Dog! That Made Him Mad' in 1956, and the remarkable 'Fujiyama Mama' in 1958. The latter song contained many references to the World War II bombing of Hiroshima and Nagasaki, yet ironically topped the charts in Japan.

The fact that she held her own on tours with Elvis, Jerry Lee Lewis, Buddy Holly and Carl Perkins was ample proof of her tough talent, but unfortunately she was simply way ahead of

31

her time. In the climate of the middle fifties, when rock 'n' roll generally was still viewed with suspicion by much of society, the chances for a girl were even more remote. 'So much of the nation wasn't accepting of Elvis and Jerry Lee and Little Richard, much less a teenage girl,' she would say.

So despite an explosively raunchy cover of Elvis's 'Let's Have a Party' in 1960 that made it into the US Top Fifty, by the early sixties she'd settled into the more predictable role model of a sentimental country singer. In 1971, as born-again Christians, Wanda and her husband/manager Wendell Goodman abandoned secular music altogether and spent the next 25 years performing gospel in churches.

Then, in 1996, Wanda Jackson was invited by 'alternative-country' singer Rosie Flores to duet with her on an upcoming album. The two were so pleased with the results that Jackson joined Flores on a handful of promotional club dates that was soon extended into a five-week North American tour. Jackson, pleasantly surprised to discover that she and her songs were known by a generation of rockabilly fans her grandchildren's age, soon put together her own band again and began touring the clubs and festivals where she continues to perform.

Recognition has come to her late in life, with honours in recent years including induction into the Rockabilly Hall of Fame and the International Hall of Fame, although her name remains conspicuously absent from the Rock 'n' Roll Hall of Fame. A new generation of artists has also acknowledged Wanda Jackson, who has recorded with the likes of the Cramps, Lee Rocker and Elvis Costello. But had things been different back in 1956, when her fiery brand of music was on a par with that of the male-dominated rock aristocracy, she could have certainly been crowned the queen of rock 'n' roll.

DON'T KNOCK THE ROCK

US, 1956–7

From the very start, rock 'n' roll came in for some hysterical criticism, mainly from teachers and preachers on both sides of the Atlantic who were convinced it was corrupting young people. Talking about the music of Elvis Presley in 1956, a New York church minister declared, 'I don't think youth wants this sort of thing. It is the result of the let-down that follows every war.'

Church officials typified the music as rebellious and satanic, warning that it would subvert American youth. As Columbia University's Dr A M Meerio was moved to conclude at the time, 'If we cannot stem the tide of rock 'n' roll with its waves of rhythmic narcosis and vicarious craze, we are preparing our own downfall in the midst of pandemic funeral dances.'

There was even a US government hearing in the mid-fifties that considered the problem rock 'n' roll music presented. At the hearing, songwriter Billy Rose (who had been responsible for the memorable lyrics, 'Barney Google, with the goo-goo-googly eyes') said he thought most of the new songs were 'Junk . . . in many cases they are obscene junk pretty much on a level with dirty comic magazines,' and described rock 'n' rollers as 'A set of untalented twisters and twitchers whose appeal is largely to the zootsuiter and the juvenile delinquent.'

Strong stuff, though at the same hearing US Congressman Emanuel Celler was more condescending: 'Rock and roll has its place, there's no question about it. It's given great impetus to talent, particularly among the colored people. It's a natural expression of their emotions and gyrations.'

A description of Elvis Presley in *Life* magazine as a 'nightmare' for which there was no room was typical of the conformist attitude toward rock 'n' roll music. Consequently, the demand arose that rock music should be banned from the radio and that DJs who ventured to spin rock 'n' roll records should be fired – which, in fact, did happen more than once. In 1958, for instance, St Louis radio station KWK had all rock 'n' roll banned from its playlist. The DJs gave every rock 'n' roll record in the station library a last spin before smashing it to pieces. The station manager said it was 'A simple weeding out of undesirable music'. There were demands that such records should also be removed from jukeboxes. Ceremonial sessions were organised in which rock 'n' roll records were publicly smashed or burned and, on quite a few occasions, local authorities prohibited live rock shows from taking place.

Reactions to rock's inexorable rise in popularity were just as passionate among those people in the music industry who had a specific interest in putting rock 'n' roll out of business. Columbia Records producer Mitch Miller, for instance, denigrated rock records as 'the comic books of music'.

But the most notorious tirade against rock music came from the Los Angeles home of crooner Frank Sinatra in a vitriolic statement published in *Western World* magazine in 1957, calling it 'The most brutal, ugly, desperate, vicious form of expression it has been my displeasure to hear,' continuing 'It smells phoney and false. It is sung, played and written for the most part by cretinous goons.' And the one-time teen idol didn't stop there: 'It manages to be the martial music of every sideburned delinquent on the face of the earth. This rancid smelling aphrodisiac I deplore.' Three years later Sinatra seemed to have changed his mind, with none other than Elvis Presley, just demobbed from the army, as the special guest on his TV show.

JAMES BROWN GOES OVER
THE TOP

NEWARK, NEW JERSEY, 1957

James Brown has been frequently been dubbed 'the Godfather of Soul', though it's a title some would dispute, maintaining that Ray Charles earned that accolade some years before Brown – Charles's unique mix of blues, gospel, R & B and jazz laying the very first foundations of what later became known as soul music. Brown also trades under the by-line 'the hardest working man in show business' and that would be a harder claim to contest, on account of his frantic stage act, first honed to a finely tuned piece of showmanship in the late fifties.

Like Ray Charles, Brown appropriated aspects of church music for his own musical ends, though in his case it was his personal delivery that was borrowed from gospel rather than the structure and arrangements of the songs themselves, as in Charles's case. Brown – whose band the Famous Flames evolved from a group called the Gospel Starlighters – was heavily influenced by such legendary 'hot gospel' shouters as Rev. Julius Cheeks of the Sensational Nightingales and Ira Tucker of the Dixie Hummingbirds. Tucker in particular was famous for what was known as 'hard singing', where the preacher would exhort the congregation with shouts and moans, often running up and down the church aisle and collapsing in ecstasy.

But although his first R & B hit came in 1956 with 'Please Please Please', James Brown's crowd-stirring act that he would similarly climax by 'collapsing' before being helped off stage, only really came into its own in the late fifties and the early sixties. There was an incident, however, when the future 'Godfather of Soul' *did* actually upstage Ray Charles (whose own 'church revival meeting' styled shows had audiences on the point of hysteria) with his extravagant showmanship, during a package show at Newark, New Jersey, sometime in 1957.

The bill was headed by Charles and rock 'n' roll star Little Richard – another 'no holds barred' performer whose stage act was legendary – and Brown, determined to excel himself in the face of such heavy competition, pulled out all the stops. The concert was held in an enormous dance hall, where the stage, far above the dance floor where the audience were standing below, was joined to a balcony at the back of the hall (where the rest of the fans were seated) by two narrow support beams.

As his act climaxed with 'Please Please Please', Brown suddenly leaped on to one of the beams, 'tightroping' across the vast space, still shouting and moaning, before collapsing into the crowd on the balcony. Even the band, well used to their leader's wild theatrics, were momentarily shaken as Brown risked injury or possibly death to get his musical message across. In terms of church-inspired theatre, it was an act that even Ray Charles and the flamboyant Little Richard would have found hard to follow.

JERRY LEE'S CHILD BRIDE

LONDON, 1958

Piano-pumping rock 'n' roller Jerry Lee Lewis is one of the great survivors of the early years of rock 'n' roll, and is now considered one of the genre's great originators. Yet in his heyday in the mid-fifties, he didn't have that many hits to his name and the main reason for the sudden halt in his fortunes after just three Top Ten chart entries was the notorious child-bride scandal in 1958.

Born in the northern Louisiana town of Ferriday on 29 September 1935, Jerry Lee Lewis grew up with music, and his parents even mortgaged their home to buy him his own piano when Jerry was just eight years old.

As a young man he studied to become a preacher at a bible college in Texas but was expelled one Sunday when – unable to resist the temptation of his musical roots – he boogied-up the hymn 'My God Is Real'. After that, he decided to dedicate himself to music.

Gradually making a name for himself on the embryo rock 'n' roll scene around America's southern states, on 21 February 1952 at the age of sixteen he got married for the first time to Dorothy Barton. It was literally a shotgun wedding; the story goes that Dorothy's brothers showed up at his door and threatened him into marrying their sister. But Jerry Lee and marriage never seemed to mix, and on 15 September 1953 he married Jane Mitcham, 23 days before his divorce with Dorothy Barton was final. In November 1954, Jane gave birth to their son, named Jerry Lee Lewis Jr.

Meanwhile, Jerry Lee had heard about Sun Records in Memphis and after making some demo sides in the studio, recorded 'Crazy Arms' in November 1956, which went on to sell a third of a million copies. He continued as a session musician at the studio, his distinctive piano style featuring on Sun classics like 'Matchbox' by Carl Perkins as well as Billy Riley's 'Red Hot' and 'Flying Saucer Rock And Roll', under his first name and last name, Jerry Lewis.

But personal stardom beckoned and, after a sensational version of 'Whole Lotta Shakin' Goin' On' sold a million copies in the summer of 1957, he was on his way. It was followed up the charts by 'Great Balls Of Fire' later that year and 'Breathless' early in 1958.

'Great Balls Of Fire' was certainly his biggest smash, making Number Two in the US charts and topping the list in the UK. But it was in England that his career would come to a sudden halt, when he went on tour there in 1958.

His marriage to Jane Mitcham had ended and on 12 December 1957 Jerry had married thirteen-year-old Myra Gale Brown, who happened to be his second cousin. Jerry didn't consider this odd because marrying distant cousins was acceptable in the South at the time, and Jerry's sister had been married at fourteen. But when Jerry Lee embarked on a tour of England in 1958, the newspapers learned about his 'child bride' – who was accompanying him on the trip – and had a field day.

The ensuing publicity caused an uproar, and the tour was cancelled after only three concerts. The rock 'n' roll star and his bemused wife were virtually drummed out of the country, and the scandal followed Jerry Lee home to America. His discs were ripped from store shelves, his appearances cancelled and his record sales declined. 'High School Confidential', from the MGM movie of the same name, sank to the bottom of the charts.

Although he was later revered as a rock 'n' roll pioneer and icon, Jerry Lee's career never really recovered from the uproar, his only hit in its aftermath being a cover version of Ray Charles's 'What'd I Say' – and that was sometime after the dust had settled, in 1961.

WHATEVER HAPPENED TO TERRY DENE?

UK, 1950s

In 1978, UK Decca Records released a compilation album of oldies ironically titled *I Thought Terry Dene was Dead*, and indeed many who remembered him from the early days of British rock 'n' roll probably thought the same. But Dene – real name Terry Williams – was alive and well, a near-forgotten name who simply couldn't handle stardom when it was thrust upon him as 'the British Elvis' in the mid-fifties.

Born in London in 1938, Dene was among the many stars that served their apprenticeship in Soho's famous 2 i's coffee bar. He was directly inspired by Elvis, and took his name from another hero, the actor James Dean. His big break came in April 1957, when he got to appear on TV for the first time in the seminal BBC rock programme *6.5 Special*, after the show's producer Jack Good had spotted him singing between bouts at a wrestling tournament. After being rejected by EMI label Columbia, Dene was signed to Decca and had three Top Twenty hits in 1957 and 1958. The first came with a cover of Marty Robbins's 'A White Sports Coat' in June 1957, followed the next month by 'Start Movin'', already a US hit for actor/singer Sal Mineo (who, coincidentally, had appeared as James Dean's sidekick in *Rebel Without a Cause* in 1955).

By 1958, with a third hit under his belt (another Marty Robbins cover, 'Stairway Of Love'), Terry Dene even starred in a movie, *The Golden Disc*. However, despite having some previous screen experience as an extra, the pressure of such sudden fame was too much for the nervously disposed singer and was not aided by the film's lack of success at the box office. He started to show symptoms of unstable behaviour, being arrested and fined for both drunkenness and vandalism.

Then came the much-publicised affair of his short-lived time in the army. Like Elvis, his management thought it could only mean good publicity when he was called up for the then-compulsory National Service, and a battery of tabloid press men were there to report his induction in 1959. However, a history of mental disturbance meant that he was released as 'medically unfit' just two months later. This time the papers had even more of a field day, hounding the troubled star and implying he was a 'wimp' compared to Elvis – and unfairly hinting that his sorry dismissal was contrived so he could return to making hit records.

Unfortunately, the kind of publicity Dene was now getting made that prospect all the more unlikely, as did the break-up of his brief marriage to the singer Edna Savage, who was another big UK name at the time. By the end of the fifties, Terry Dene's career as a pop star had effectively come to an end and in the early sixties he 'saw the light' in a conversion to evangelical religion, knocking on people's doors and singing in the street.

There followed twenty years of active evangelism, including several albums for religious labels including *If That isn't Love* and *Call to the Winds*, both on Pilgrim. The Decca compilation *I Thought Terry Dene was Dead* followed a biography of the same name by Dan Wooding, published in 1974.

Then, in the early eighties, Terry Dene returned to live rock in the rock 'n' roll revival that was happening at the time, playing pubs and clubs backed by members of his original group the Dene-Aces. His live performances were always more exciting than his somewhat derivative records, and he was welcomed back by many UK fans of vintage rock 'n' roll as if he had, indeed, come back from the dead.

ELVIS'S TRAVELS

GERMANY, 1958

Considering that Elvis Presley, along with the Beatles, was the biggest rock 'n' roll star of all time and sold records in every country in the world (including the Soviet Union where they were officially banned), it's a strange fact of history that he actually played no live dates outside North America – except for Hawaii, which in any case is part of the United States.

In fact, Elvis never travelled much at all; his only trip to Europe was in 1958 when he was posted to Germany during his army service. During that trip he did make a journey to Paris when on a short leave, and actually stopped off at Prestwick airport in Scotland, due to bad weather on his journey home in March 1960. Tour-wise, his record-breaking treks took him over the Canadian border a handful of times for concerts that included Toronto, Ottawa and Vancouver, but that was about it.

At the time, the excuse most often given was that the star didn't like flying, though offers to ship him to a European date in a luxury liner were also apparently turned down. But the real background to the King's refusal to travel abroad was the fact that his manager Colonel Tom Parker simply didn't want him to. And the root of *that* mystery – why would the manager of the highest-profile star in the world turn down multimillion-dollar engagements – lay in the fact that the self-styled 'Colonel' didn't have his own passport.

According to Parker himself he was born in West Virginia, 1910, from where, after being orphaned as a child, he ran away and joined the circus – the circus in question being the Great Parker Pony Circus owned by his uncle. From there he drifted into carnival work and small-time showbiz before seizing his chance when he got the young Elvis to sign on the dotted line.

But the correct version of Tom Parker's murky history gives his real name as Andreas Kujik who, it seems, entered the United States illegally from his native Holland in the thirties. According to an unsubstantiated story, he was actually on the run from the Dutch police following the unsolved murder of a woman in his home town.

Whatever the real story, it was certainly Tom Parker's stubbornness on the subject that meant that the most famous name in popular music never really travelled (apart from his brief hops to Canada) to any country outside his own.

THE UNCROWNED KING OF
ROCK 'N' ROLL SAXOPHONE

NEW YORK CITY, 1958–9

One of the most familiar sounds in rock 'n' roll was that of a saxophone player who was never credited on his most famous appearances on vinyl.

Curtis Ousley, better known as King Curtis, began playing tenor sax with the jazz bandleader Lionel Hampton in the late forties, before playing recording-session dates for Nat King Cole, Buddy Holly, Brook Benton and many more. And most famously, in many of the house bands assembled at Atlantic Records throughout the fifties, backing the likes of Joe Turner, LaVern Baker, the Drifters and the Coasters.

It was with the vocal group the Coasters that Curtis, through 1958 and 1959, created a musical trademark of the period. His snappy 'yakkety sax' solos matched perfectly the group's zany teen-wise songs (almost all of which were penned by Jerry Leiber and Mike Stoller), including 'Charlie Brown', 'Along Came Jones' and most memorably 'Yaketty Yak', an eternal anthem for put-down adolescents everywhere. Yet, as has been the lot of thousands of session musicians throughout pop music's history, his name never appeared on these records that most famously bore his mark.

From the early sixties, Curtis began making records under his own name and through the decade had over a dozen instrumental hits in the American charts. He also played backing on records and live dates for numerous stars of the era, including the Beatles, Aretha Franklin, Wilson Pickett and

John Lennon – but now with his name firmly on the personnel list.

In August 1971 Curtis was returning home to his apartment on West 86th Street in New York City; it was heatwave time, and the saxophone star was carrying a new air-conditioning unit he had just purchased. Struggling from his car to the building, he found his way to the door blocked by two junkies, who were injecting heroin there on the front steps. When he asked them to move a fight ensued, during which 37-year-old Curtis was stabbed in the heart with a stiletto. He was dead by the time he reached the hospital.

His funeral was a star-studded affair, with Jesse Jackson delivering the sermon and Aretha Franklin singing a hymn. In the latter years of a life tragically cut short, King Curtis had been recognised as one of the great rhythm and blues saxophone players, despite his greatest contribution to rock 'n' roll being unacknowledged when it was first actually made.

A FOLK-ROCK MOVER AND SHAKER

NEW YORK CITY, 1958-66

The history of rock 'n' roll music is littered with the names of almost-forgotten 'movers and shakers' of their day – musicians, singers, record producers and others who exerted a significant impact on developments around them. One such name is that of Richard Fariña, an early influence on the folk-rock movement that was spearheaded by the young Bob Dylan.

His mother Irish, his father Cuban, Fariña was brought up in the comfortable Flatbush area of Brooklyn. A born romantic, his oft-repeated accounts of an adventurous life in the fifties involving Ernest Hemingway, the IRA, the Cuban Revolution and such, were something of an exaggeration in contrast to the reality of a successful engineering student who progressed from Brooklyn High School of Technology to Cornell University. While at Cornell he developed literary ambitions, openly acknowledging his major influences as Hemingway and the Welsh poet Dylan Thomas, and transferred from engineering to a creative writing course at the end of 1957.

His first post-college job brought him to Manhattan, working in an ad agency, where he began to frequent the literary haunts around Greenwich Village, including particularly the White Horse Tavern on Hudson Street, where Dylan Thomas had famously drunk his last drop and died in a stupor back in 1953. The White Horse had also been a watering hole for other writers including Norman Mailer, Lawrence Ferlinghetti and Jack Kerouac; Fariña was in his element.

He very soon got embroiled in the Greenwich Village folk scene. He'd got to know the influential singer Dave Van Ronk after a chance meeting at Allan Block's Sandal Shop on West 4th Street, where musicians and anyone interested in folk would hang out, talking music, busking songs – buying sandals usually being the last thing on their mind. David Hajdu recalls the incident in his scholarly account of that period, *Positively 4th Street*. Van Ronk was strumming a banjo – which he couldn't play – when a voice from the other side of the shop commented loudly, 'You know, you can't play the banjo, but you're the best banjo player I've ever heard!' The comments came from Fariña.

When Gerde's Folk City – one of the most important venues on the New York folk scene – opened in May 1960, Fariña was there, as was singer Carolyn Hester, the guest performer that night. Fariña was captivated by Hester's striking beauty and personality; they dated, and in less than three weeks were married. He learned to play the dulcimer from his wife and began songwriting.

However, Carolyn Hester was a moving spirit in her own right long before she met Richard Fariña. She had been part of the Village coffee-house circuit since the mid-fifties, touring with the seminal folk outfit the New Lost City Ramblers. Her eponymous third album on Columbia (but first for a major label) was significant for not only solidly establishing her as part of a 'new' folk tradition, but because it also featured a then-unknown Bob Dylan on harmonica, just a year before his own debut on the same label.

But the marriage was doomed almost from the start, or certainly from the start of Richard's musical ambitions. He took on the role of 'creative consultant' to his wife's increasing professional activity, which included cutting the record for Columbia, an involvement Hester was later to recall was largely uninvited. Likewise, when he made a trip to London where he picked up gigs around the folk clubs there, his wife joined him a few weeks later and found they were billed at various venues as a duo – something she insists she never planned.

Nevertheless, Fariña's songwriting was producing results,

including his debut album, which was made in 1963 during the London sojourn with Ric von Schmidt, and included Bob Dylan under his oft-used pseudonym (for contractual reasons) of 'Blind Boy Grunt'. The album featured some Fariña originals including the anti-bomb protest 'Christmas Island'.

(Eric) von Schmidt was himself a veteran of the folk scene, having come to Manhattan via the same Cambridge, Massachusetts student circuit as singer Joan Baez; a fine painter and blues guitar player, von Schmidt was one of the best-known characters around the Greenwich Village clubs. His name was to become familiar around the world after 1962 when Bob Dylan featured one of his songs – 'Baby Let Me Follow You Down' – on his first album, and namechecked the composer in his spoken introduction – 'I met him one day in the green pastures of Harvard University.'

Richard's marriage with Carolyn was finished by 1964, not long after which Fariña became involved with – and eventually married – Joan Baez's younger sister Mimi, also a fine singer and rising name in her own right in the folk revival. Together, Mimi and Fariña produced important songs and albums, including *Celebration of a Grey Day* (with some of his best known compositions 'Reno Nevada' and 'Pack Up Your Sorrows') and *Reflections in a Crystal Wind*.

His life came to an abrupt and tragic end when he was killed in a motorcycle accident on the eve of the launch party for his book *Been Down So Long, It Looks Like Up To Me* in 1966. Whatever may be judged about the undoubted opportunism in many of Richard Fariña's career moves, he was a genuine 'mover and shaker' on the Greenwich Village scene who was a pioneer spirit in the burgeoning folk-rock movement that followed.

THE DAY THE MUSIC DIED

MASON CITY, IOWA, 1959

When Buddy Holly was killed in the fatal plane crash that also claimed the lives of Richie Valens and the Big Bopper on 3 February 1959, it was almost inevitable that some weird stories would appear in the aftermath of the tragedy.

The stars had been playing a date in Clear Lake, Iowa, and Holly had chartered a small plane to take himself and others on to the next date in Moorhead, Minnesota. Bad weather brought the aircraft down in a field just eight miles from where it had taken off in Mason City, the nearest airport to Clear Lake, killing all three rock idols and the 21-year-old pilot, Roger Peterson.

Years later a gun was found at the site of the crash, which turned out to have belonged to Holly. However, when the farmer who found the weapon spoke to the press, his comments that it was still in perfect condition were reported instead as it having been 'fired recently'. That in turn was misread by many as meaning it had been fired recently before the crash, fuelling a rumour that Holly had shot Peterson – either in anger or by accident – causing the plane to plummet to the ground. None of this was borne out by the coroner's reports after the fatalities of course, but that didn't prevent the story doing the rounds.

More bizarrely, there was a myth going round that Holly had survived the accident, hideously scarred, and was living out his life in hiding with a secret identity. And when Don McLean had his 1971 hit 'American Pie', said to be inspired by Holly's death ('the day the music died'), a story emerged that the plane was actually called 'Miss American Pie', echoed in the chorus of the song, although there was no truth in it.

What was scary however, was the fate that almost befell Holly's guitarist and bass player, Waylon Jennings and Tommy Allsup, both destined to be country-music stars in their own right. Holly had allotted the spare seats in the aircraft to the two backing musicians, before J P Richardson – the Big Bopper – persuaded Jennings to let him take his seat, complaining that the long bus ride ahead was particularly uncomfortable for a man of his size. Likewise, Richie Valens was angling for a place on the plane, although Tommy Allsup was reluctant to give up his seat. Eventually they decided to toss for it. Allsup agreed to the deal so long as he could have Richardson's sleeping bag if he lost and had to ride the bus. The Bopper said OK, Allsup flipped a coin, and Valens shouted 'Heads'. And heads it was.

MOONDOG ON THE STREETS OF NEW YORK

NEW YORK CITY, 1950s–60s

A seminal influence on the 'underground' scene of sixties rock music was a New York musician whose music was also experienced by literally thousands of ordinary New Yorkers, who heard him playing live almost every day of every year through the fifties and sixties.

He called himself Moondog, and was a spectacular regular fixture on Sixth Avenue between 52nd and 56th Streets. Indeed, the corner of Sixth and 54th became known as Moondog Corner, as that was where he most often entertained passers-by – playing his compositions on home-made instruments and reciting his own poetry. An imposing figure, Moondog was all the more noticeable due to his long beard, flowing robe, leather patchwork trousers and Viking helmet; he was also usually carrying a tall spear.

But few of the people who saw the blind musician (he wasn't a busker, he didn't ask for donations) on their way to and from the office every day would have suspected that he was an accomplished recording artist, with albums of symphonic music and spoken poetry on his backlist, some even recorded right there on the streets of Manhattan.

Born Louis Thomas Hardin in Maryville, Kansas in 1916, the self-taught street player first appeared on the Prestige label in the fifties with *Caribea* (which featured added percussion and tap-dancing!), *More Moondog* and *The Story of Moondog*. Among the bohemian 'beat generation' community, his records achieved cult status, none more so than *On the Streets of New York*, an EP recorded *in situ*.

The original sleeve notes from the UK release on the London label gave some idea of the flavour of the sound therein: 'The music heard in the EP is the result of recording and editing several hours of taped music in order to cull the most unusual. In this record, Moondog plays several new instruments – the "oo", the "utsu", and the "samisen". In one composition, recorded near the Hudson River piers, tugboat and ocean liner whistles and foghorns complement the composition, while Moondog plays and improvises; another work similarly uses the actual sounds of New York traffic – automobile motors, taxi horns, sounds of brakes, etc.'

In addition to more bizarre instruments, Moondog could also play piano, organ, clarinet and most other woodwind and string instruments, while his wife Suzuko was capable of singing in three octaves and figured prominently in some of his recordings.

Moondog came under an unexpected blaze of publicity when he successfully took the pioneering rock 'n' roll DJ Alan Freed to court, forcing the latter to drop the name Moondog from his radio show *Moondog's Rock 'n' Roll Party*. Later, in 1969, Columbia Records producer James Guercio (best known for albums by rock bands Blood Sweat & Tears and Chicago) approached Moondog on the street. This resulted in the orchestral LP *Moondog*, a work that hovered between jazz and classical music.

In the mid-seventies, Moondog moved to Germany, where he continued to compose highly experimental works, including the 1995 *Big Band* album and *Sax Pax for a Sax* in 1997. His influence on the avant-garde end of rock music was considerable, and the impact of his lifestyle on the New York beat and underground scene highly significant. Janis Joplin even covered one of his Prestige tracks, 'All Is Loneliness', with Big Brother and the Holding Company in the sixties. Moondog died in 2001.

THE BEATNIK HORROR

LIVERPOOL, 1960

As long as there have been 'teenagers' – a term that only came into common usage in the fifties – there has been a tabloid media eager to warn society of miscreant youth's latest transgression. That was as true in the case of the first 'juvenile delinquents' as it is now with the latest exposé of some post-punk pop star popping pills or smoking a joint. 'The young are revolting,' has always had a double-edged resonance as a newspaper story.

In late-fifties Britain, however, rock 'n' roll had become something of a lame duck as far as sensation-seeking journalists were concerned. Things had certainly got tamer with the nation's number one faves Cliff Richard and the Shadows – a long way from 'Tutti Frutti', 'Hound Dog' and 'Great Balls Of Fire'. Little wonder then that scandal-starved scribblers looked elsewhere for shock-horror headlines, finding the answer to their search in the unwashed, besandaled subculture known as beatnik.

The name had its origin in the USA and was a derogatory reference to the 'Beat Generation' writers – Ginsberg, Kerouac *et al.* – and their youthful followers. The '-nik' suffix, culled from the Russian 'Sputnik' satellite that had beaten the Americans into the space race, became instantly derisory – and has ever since stayed part of the language, from 'peacenik' to 'refusenik'.

It was perhaps inevitable then, when in 1960 the *Sunday People* newspaper ran a series exposing the latest danger to the nation's youth under the heading 'The Beatnik Horror!' Visiting various cities and towns across the country, each episode of the weekly revelations focused on another group of long-haired malcontents; the issue that appeared on 24 July turned its spotlight of shame on Liverpool.

On their arrival in Liverpool and seeking out the local bohemia, the *People* reporters had been pointed in the direction of Allan Williams, the black-bearded owner of the Jacaranda coffee bar. The 'Jac' as it was known locally was a regular rendezvous of the art student population and their hangers-on, so Williams was certainly the man to talk to. Possibly to garner publicity for his own enterprises or, as later rumour had it, in return for a cash hand-out, Williams arranged for the hacks to visit the occupants of 3 Hilary Mansions. There, in a run-down Georgian dwelling in the once-grand Gambier Terrace, just round the corner from the Art College, a scene of 'decadent squalor' met their eyes – though, it transpired, not quite sordid enough for the requirements of the journalists.

The flat was rented by art student Rod Murray, who shared it with a colleague from the painting school, Stuart Sutcliffe. A third art-school crony would occasionally stay there, when he wanted to spend the night with his girlfriend Cynthia, away from the suburban home where he lived with his aunt. His name was John Lennon. The three had been joined by various other friends, eager to get their pictures in the paper 'for a laugh'. The journalists arrived and announced they were writing an article on how hard it was to survive on student grants. Lennon agreed with them, according to Rod Murray, telling them he had to 'go home and scrounge meals from his relatives'.

Just so things would look a little more desperate, the newspapermen suggested – as they handed out drinks to the grateful students – that they rough the place up a little, making it look more of a hovel than it actually was. So old papers, empty cups and so on were strewn around the place which, along with the bare light bulbs and paint-spattered floorboards, made the desired slum-like effect.

When the *Sunday People* appeared, parents and relatives of

the youngsters involved were furious – so this was how their offspring lived when away from home – despite protestations by the students that they'd been set up. One of the 'beatniks' was quoted as saying he'd managed to avoid the National Service draft into the forces 'by posing as a psychiatric case', another that they sought happiness through meditation. Claiming that 'they revel in filth', the article went on to describe the beatniks' 'free love' lifestyle, which was then taboo in respectable society; it observed there were 'not really orgies – but they get very naughty', and concluded the kids were 'on the road to hell'.

The picture that accompanied the article showed Allan Williams and the students lounging around the floor; in the background, various road signs and other items of street furniture were used as part of the unconventional décor. Prominent in the picture, with long Elvis-style sideburns and wearing sunglasses, was John Lennon – the first time, but certainly not the last, that his picture would appear in a national newspaper.

KILLED BY THE KLAN

HOPE, ARKANSAS, 1960

Vocalist Jesse Belvin was one of the unsung heroes of rock 'n' roll, who met his end in tragic and controversial circumstances. He co-wrote one of the biggest smashes of the fifties, 'Earth Angel', which was a hit for the Penguins in 1955. Belvin's recording of 'Goodnight My Love' was used by Dick Clark as the closing theme for the seminal *American Bandstand* TV show for several years, and he made the US pop charts in 1959 with 'Guess Who'. But his potential was far greater than these statistics would suggest, a sweet-voiced crooner in the Nat King Cole style who could also out-raunch Elvis when he wanted to. Indeed, it was his sensational emulation of Presley and Little Richard that caused RCA Records to sign Belvin and begin a unique promotion in 1959.

It was in the formative years of the civil rights movement, and RCA wanted badly to tap into the segregated South, by offering a 'Black Elvis'. This in itself was ironic, as early promotional material for Presley (from the same company) often called him 'The White Soul Singer' or 'A White Little Richard'.

Belvin had been playing the very first integrated pop concert in Little Rock, Arkansas on 6 February 1960. It had been a far from comfortable experience, with white supremacists twice managing to halt the show, shouting racial abuse and urging the white teenagers in attendance to leave at once. There had also been at least six death threats on Belvin just prior to the show so when it was over Belvin sped away from Arkansas as quickly as possible. Then, as the singer's black Cadillac passed through Hope, Arkansas, it skidded off the road, the horrific smash killing Jesse and his driver instantly. His wife JoAnn died later from her injuries at the Hope Hospital.

As word reached the black community in Belvin's home town of Los Angeles, there were immediately rumours of foul play. And the fact that Belvin had phoned his mother twice in the last three days, every time telling her about the hostile receptions he received, made suspicions even stronger: he rarely called home from the road, and never more than once a month.

Speculation was confirmed when one of the first state troopers on the accident scene stated that both of the rear tyres on Belvin's car had been 'obviously tampered with'. He gave no more details, but it was clear that the local 'Ku Klux Klan' bigots were almost certainly responsible for the horrific fatalities, and the death of a true rock 'n' roll original.

DAVID BOWIE'S EYES

BROMLEY, KENT, 1960

Fans of David Bowie have long pondered over why the singer has one eye a different colour to the other. It was caused by an injury that he sustained to his left eye while still at school in Bromley. Aged thirteen, David Jones, as he then was, had got into a fight over a girl, with a friend called George Underwood.

After the fight David had to spend over four months in hospital, and was in danger of losing the sight of the eye completely. Eventually he was left with an enlarged pupil in the left eye. This still shows basically hazel, compared to the natural blue of his right eye.

The blow from Underwood that did the damage was delivered with his bare fist, although later sensationalist accounts (which began to circulate years later when Bowie had become a superstar) variously claimed he had been injured with a toy airplane propeller, or even a pair of geometry compasses! But all's well that ends well: Bowie and his playground rival Underwood later played in groups together, and have remained firm friends ever since.

THE BIRTH OF THE TWIST

PHILADELPHIA, 1960

There was a fashion for dance crazes in the early sixties, ranging from the Hully Gully to the Locomotion, but the dance that stood out from all the rest, and swept the world as a consequence, was one that could be done by folks who couldn't actually dance – the Twist. This dance was described as someone stubbing a cigarette out with one foot while at the same time swinging their hips, with their arms rocking side to side as if towelling their back after a shower.

The original Twist record, simply entitled 'The Twist', was released by Hank Ballard and the Midnighters in 1959. Ballard was booked to plug the record on the Philadelphia-based Dick Clark TV show *American Bandstand*, but when the singer didn't turn up for the broadcast, ex-chicken-plucker Chubby Checker (real name Ernest Evans) got the gig.

Local boy Checker had signed with the Cameo Parkway label the previous year, on the recommendation of Dick Clark's wife, and when he was offered the *Bandstand* spot quickly recorded the number with the TV studio's band. The resulting version was a smash in 1960, hitting the Number One spot in the US charts. It charted again the following year, along with its equally popular follow-up 'Let's Twist Again', after which the dance took off worldwide as a genuine craze.

The original live-venue catalyst for the fad was a New York club – the Peppermint Lounge on West 45th Street, where the house band was the Starlighters, fronted by Italian-American singer Joey Dee. The group had the follow-up hit to Checker's

1961 'Twist' chart entries with 'Peppermint Twist', and the club was an instant magnet for socialites, the good and the glam flocking to the place where 'the Twist was born'. Dee's only other Top Ten hit was 'Shout', and both were included on his hit LP *Twist at the Peppermint Lounge*. The Starlighters, however, was the launch pad for The Ronettes, who were Dee's dancers and backing singers until they were discovered by Phil Spector; the Starlighters also included, at various stages, three of the four original Young Rascals, guitarist Jimi Hendrix and movie actor to-be Joe Pesci.

JIMI JUMPS OUT

FORT CAMPBELL, KENTUCKY, 1961

After playing in local bands in his home town of Seattle as a teenager, James Marshall Hendrix – later to be known as Jimi Hendrix – enlisted in the US Army at the age of eighteen. There in 1961 he joined the wonderfully named Screaming Eagles paratroops squad based at Fort Campbell, Kentucky, but on his 26th parachute jump broke his ankle. Because of his accident he was discharged and after just fourteen months in the forces he went back into the music game and made rock 'n' roll history as a guitar superstar.

That's the official story. But a recent biographer claimed that in fact the musician, regretting he'd joined up and feeling the urge to return to making music, pretended to be gay in order to be demobbed from the service.

The author Charles Cross claimed he'd unearthed military medical reports, which supported the notion that although Hendrix had indeed been injured, he'd faked his way out of the army using the 'gay' scam. These included copies of documents he said had been filed by psychiatrists who saw Hendrix while he was enlisted, following which Captain John Halbert recommended that Hendrix be discharged because of his 'homosexual tendencies'.

If indeed his discharge was the result of an audacious con trick on the part of the guitarist, or just a bad landing as he glided to earth on a parachute jump, Jimi Hendrix leaving the army at that point in his life was certainly a case of Uncle Sam's loss being rock 'n' roll's gain.

HAMMOND'S FOLLY: THE EARLY ODYSSEY OF BOB DYLAN

NEW YORK CITY, 1962

The streets of Hibbing, a small town up by the Canadian border in Northern Minnesota, may seem a million miles from the car-horn echoing canyons of Manhattan. But for any kid in the mid-fifties hung up on rock 'n' roll, New York City, with its skyline straight out of the movies, simply *was* rock 'n' roll – and sixteen-year-old Robert Zimmerman was certainly hung up on rock 'n' roll.

Born in 1941, he was nearly fifteen – just the right age – when Elvis's 'Heartbreak Hotel' was released on an unsuspecting world. Zimmerman already had a passion for music; the late country star Hank Williams had been a hero for some years, and he picked up on all the sounds coming across on the radio be it gospel, blues, 'hillbilly' music or straight pre-rock pop songs. But for a while, it was rock that captured his attention most.

By the time Bob Zimmerman entered the University of Minnesota in Minneapolis however, he had moved from being an amateur rock 'n' roll singer (he'd even had a short-lived group, the Rock Boppers) to amateur folk singer, by then the music of choice in college fraternities across America. The folk-song revival was under way and, with an enthusiasm bordering on the evangelical – which had previously characterised his passion for the early rock 'n' rollers – Bob Dillon as he now called himself (after the original TV cowboy character Matt Dillon) was determined to be a part of it, one hundred per cent.

His college studies soon gave way to living the bohemian existence of the student-turned-beatnik, moving into the arty quarter of Dinkytown and performing regularly at local coffee houses and such. His repertoire was dominated by the 'contemporary' material of the folk revival – songs popularised by Pete Seeger, Harry Belafonte, Odetta and, most importantly, Woody Guthrie.

Guthrie became the next big fixation of Dylan's teenage life (who'd by now changed the spelling of his adopted surname to match Welsh poet Dylan Thomas and also because 'it looked better'). The impact of Guthrie's songs on the young singer was complemented by his romantic lifestyle as narrated in his 1941 'on the road' biography *Bound for Glory*. This chronicle, which Dylan read as his 'Bible' for a time, was to be a prime inspiration in the latter's decision to hitchhike east to visit his ailing hero in New York. Eventually, after minor setbacks, Dylan hit Manhattan in the company of a fellow singer David Underhill, who hailed from the city. It was January 1961, and almost right away the youngster became a fixture on the Greenwich Village folk-club scene, playing at the Café Wha?, the Gaslight and Mills Tavern, in fact anywhere that would let him do a set.

By September of that year Dylan was being noticed enough to warrant a review in the *New York Times* by resident folk critic Robert Shelton, who wrote: 'A bright new face in folk music is appearing at Gerde's Folk City. Although only twenty years old, Bob Dylan is one of the most distinctive stylists to play in a Manhattan cabaret in months.'

At the same time, as planned, Dylan was visiting the increasingly fragile Guthrie at Greystone Park Psychiatric Hospital in New Jersey, his home at Coney Island and later the Brooklyn State Hospital. According to some observers, he took on a Woody Guthrie persona in many ways, affecting a singer-as-hobo look and even including a self-penned 'Song To Woody' on his first album, after being 'discovered' on the Greenwich Village scene (largely via the Shelton review) by Columbia Records' legendary producer John Hammond.

Initial reactions to Dylan's debut album, released early in

1962 and simply called *Bob Dylan*, were mixed; folk fans were divided over it, and to the public at large it meant little or nothing. It went unnoticed by many reviewers, but those that covered it thought it 'unusual' or 'interesting'; one notorious comment from a Columbia salesman described it as 'a piece of shit'. Another called it 'Hammond's Folly', and his conviction that the veteran producer had made a serious mistake seemed to be supported by the sales figures.

The album only sold about five thousand copies in that first year, and Hammond had to fight to keep Dylan under contract with the company. But its mix of standard folk numbers, blues and one original, 'Song To Woody', stood apart from contemporary folk releases by virtue of the unusual voice and delivery. It instantly became a cult record, and represented for Bobby Zimmerman a vindication of the teenage odyssey that had taken him from a small town in Minnesota to the bustling streets of Manhattan.

THE 'ANONYMOUS' DARLENE LOVE

LOS ANGELES, 1962

Like many singers who have worked in an anonymous 'session' capacity in the recording studios, Darlene Love's contribution has gone unacknowledged on scores of recordings. But as well as appearing on more than two dozen chart hits, she must hold some kind of record for being a member of two charting groups simultaneously, while at the same time enjoying hits under her own name.

Born Darlene Wright on 26 July 1941 in Los Angeles, she was raised by religious parents, the Rev. Joe and Ellen Wright, along with three brothers and a sister named Edna (who later gained fame as lead singer of the Honey Cone). Darlene was inspired to sing by listening to her mother's records of Marion Anderson and joined the St Paul Baptist Church Choir at the age of seventeen, before which time she had already joined a local group called the Echoes, in 1957.

She was approached by a member of an all-girl vocal group called the Blossoms, who asked her to come and sing at her wedding, and this turned out to be more of an audition to see if she could replace one of the girls who was leaving. At the time the line-up of the Blossoms was Gloria Jones, Fanita Barrett, Nanette and her sister Annette Williams, whose place Darlene would take. Nanette dropped out of the group soon after, and as a trio the Blossoms (with Darlene singing lead) would become known as 'the most successful unknown group of the sixties' after singing backing on hits as diverse as Bobby Day's million seller 'Rockin' Robin' (their first chart hit, in 1958),

Sam Cooke's 'Everybody Likes To Cha Cha Cha' and 'Chain Gang', Shelley Fabares's 'Johnny Angel', Duane Eddy's 'Dance With The Guitar Man', James Darren's 'Goodbye Cruel World' and Bobby 'Boris' Pickett's 'Monster Mash'.

In 1962 Darlene had a phone call from Lester Sill (whom the Blossoms had done some sessions with), who at the time was in partnership with Phil Spector. (He and Spector had founded the Philles label, named after the first letters of their respective names). They wanted Darlene to record 'He's A Rebel', a cover of a song by Vicky Carr, which they had originally earmarked for a Brooklyn group called the Crystals. Spector was in a panic when the New York outfit wouldn't come to LA because they were afraid of flying, but in his rush to beat the Carr version into the charts he didn't have time to change the name so the single went out as the Crystals – and into the Number One spot, selling over a million copies.

At this point, Darlene was actually in competition with herself – the Crystals' October chart-topper was preceded at Number One by 'Monster Mash', a song she had sung background on along with the other Blossoms. Then, amazingly, she was back in the Top Five almost immediately as a member of another Spector 'group', Bobby Soxx the Blue Jeans, with 'Zip-a Dee Doo-Dah'!

Next Darlene was to record another song for Phil Spector, 'He's Sure The Boy I Love', this time under her own name – or at least as she'd been rechristened as Darlene Love instead of Darlene Wright. She would continue to record more classics for the Philles label as Darlene Love including '(Today I Met) The Boy I'm Going to Marry', 'Wait Till My Bobby Gets Home', 'A Fine Fine Boy' and the marvellous 'Playing For Keeps'. In fact the week in May 1963 that she dented the charts with '(Today I Met) The Boy I'm Going to Marry', Darlene was also up there with the Crystals and the classic 'Da Doo Ron Ron'.

As a solo session singer and member of the Blossoms, Darlene Love continued to grace the charts, albeit anonymously, on hits that ranged from 'You've Lost That Lovin' Feeling' and 'Unchained Melody' by the Righteous

Brothers, to Ike and Tina Turner's 'River Deep – Mountain High' and 'That's Life' by Frank Sinatra. The Blossoms were even featured as a backing group for Elvis Presley for a time in the early seventies.

Darlene Love has continued to work into the 21st century, although now more often than not under her own name – at the time of writing she was in the Broadway cast of the musical *Hairspray*. And she still holds the record for featuring in the charts under three different names simultaneously, back in the early sixties when she was an all-but 'unknown' backing singer.

THE SACKING OF PETE BEST

LIVERPOOL, 1962

Drummer Pete Best was one of the foundation stones of the Beatles. He'd struggled with them when they were the Silver Beatles playing seedy dives in Hamburg. His mother Mona had let the group rehearse in her Liverpool club the Casbah. He had been with them as they built up a huge local following at the Cavern Club, and was as popular as John, Paul and George due to his affable personality and good looks. He was a signatory of the management contract with Brian Epstein, experienced the same let-down when the group was rejected by Decca and other record companies, and was with them when EMI producer George Martin took an interest in the group for a possible single on the Parlophone label.

It was then, in the summer of 1962, just when they seemed on the verge of 'making it' with a recording contract, that Pete was called to Brian Epstein's office and told that his three colleagues had decided he should leave. He was devastated. Epstein – it seems his fellow Beatles couldn't face him themselves – had the thankless task of telling Pete that 'the boys' wanted Ringo Starr in and him out. There was no explanation as to why, that was simply what had been decided, and in the aftermath of the Beatles' subsequent success Pete Best's fate that day became one of the all-time hard-luck sagas of rock 'n' roll.

The ferociously loyal Liverpool fans were as stunned as 21-year-old Pete. He was as integral a part of the Beatles as the others; nobody could understand why he'd been axed, especially right then. Various theories as to the reasons behind his dismissal started to circulate. One was that he wouldn't 'flatten' his slick quiff into the embryo 'mop top' style adopted by the other three. Another was that he was, in the view of Lennon, McCartney and Harrison, becoming too popular with the fans. A third notion pinned the blame on their new-found record producer Martin, who allegedly offered to sign the group on the condition that they changed drummers.

None of these hypotheses were ever proven, but there was probably an element of all three in the decision to give Pete Best the sack. What is known is that he was indeed as popular with the fans as his colleagues, and at the time his hairstyle did look a bit 'teddy boy' and out of date compared to the others' trendy cuts.

It's also on record that George Martin said he'd sign the band, but didn't think Best was good enough to appear on their records, he'd get a session musician for that – but he never gave the group a 'sack Pete or forget it' ultimatum. Indeed, on their debut single 'Love Me Do', Martin used a session player, Andy White, rather than Pete's replacement Ringo Starr, though Ringo would play on the later recording of the song that appeared on their first album *Please Please Me* in February 1963.

Ringo, who was well known to all four Beatles as part of Rory Storm and the Hurricanes, had been approached by George, Paul and John weeks before Pete was unceremoniously given the devastating news. That was delivered in Brian Epstein's office on 16 August 1962 after the drummer had been summoned there with a naturally nervous Neil Aspinall, the group's road manager. The other Beatles were nowhere around when the news was broken, the whole episode seeming all the more shoddy because they delegated the responsibility, leaving all the 'dirty work' to others.

'We were cowards when we sacked him,' John Lennon would later admit. 'We made Brian do it. But if we'd told Pete to his face, that would have been much nastier than getting Brian to do it. It would probably have ended up in a fight if we'd told him.'

Once the news of what would be the most famous sacking in rock history broke, the Beatles' Liverpool following was in disarray. Did they side with Pete as the unfairly dealt-with injured party, or stay loyal to the group who they were all convinced – rightly so as it happens – were on the verge of making it very big?

Although most of the fans ultimately followed the latter course, cheering the band on like a local football team as they went on to conquer the world of pop music, there was one mark of the dissension in the fans' ranks that can still be seen today. Many Best fans rallied to Pete's support when he left, picketing outside the Cavern and shouting slogans like 'Pete for ever, Ringo never' and 'Pete is Best'. Then, when the Beatles made their first appearance at the club with new drummer Ringo, an angry Pete Best loyalist threw a punch at George Harrison as the four descended the steps into the basement venue; and still visible today, on a promotional photograph taken at the EMI studios in London a couple of days later, is the black eye the guitarist sustained as a result.

BOB ON THE BEEB

LONDON, 1962

The first time that Bob Dylan ever set foot outside the United States was to appear in a long-forgotten play on BBC television in London, playing the part of a folk-singing student. It was towards the end of 1962, his first album had been released just a few months earlier, and he was a leading light on New York's Greenwich Village folk scene – but nowhere much else. It came as something of a surprise, therefore, when a British TV director, Philip Saville, approached the young Dylan after seeing him perform in one of the Village folk clubs.

Saville thought the tousle-haired beatnik would be perfect for the role of an anarchist student in *Madhouse on Castle Street*, and after some brief negotiations with Bob's manager Albert Grossman he secured a deal. Dylan was flown to London, where he stayed at Saville's home in genteel Hampstead, but soon found himself roaming the capital's thriving folk clubs. People still have misty recollections of him getting up to sing at now-legendary venues like the Troubadour, the King and Queen, and the Singer's Club – a folk evening in the Pindar of Wakefield pub on Grays Inn Road run by Ewan MacColl (a leading figure in British folk music and father of Kirsty MacColl).

It took Saville all his time to keep track of his house guest, who came and went at the oddest hours, ate meals at three in the morning and, Saville recalled, 'smoked a lot of pot'. On one occasion, when Bob seemed to have gone missing, Saville eventually found him passed out underneath a car two streets away. Another morning, not long after dawn, the BBC man awoke to the sound of Dylan serenading his two Spanish au pair girls with 'Blowin' In The Wind', which had yet to appear on record.

Things didn't get any better when rehearsals started at the television studios. The play, by Jamaican playwright Evan Jones, called for an 'anarchic young student who wrote songs', but Bob proved more anarchic than Saville had planned for. He would invariably arrive late, had trouble remembering lines and disappeared frequently to smoke a joint. When he did get to his lines, he would mumble weird improvisations instead of what was in the script.

As his lines were reduced, those assigned to actor David Warner increased, who virtually took over the role of the youthful anarchist, leaving Dylan to play himself – a guy called Bobby who sang songs. 'He gave the impression of being hopelessly lost,' Warner would recall later. 'No one had the slightest idea why he had been sent there. When he started singing, it began to become clear.'

Dylan ended up speaking one line on the screen: 'Well, I don't know – I'll have to go home and think about it,' but Saville had obviously been impressed by Bob's early-morning rendition of 'Blowin' In The Wind' – the play opened and closed with Dylan performing the song. Like Dylan's appearances at those London folk venues, the broadcast – though well received at the time – is now a fading memory, as the BBC wiped the tapes (as was normal practice in those days) soon after transmission on 12 January 1963.

More than forty years later, the fading memory of *Madhouse on Castle Street* hit the TV screens again in a BBC documentary. Entitled *Dylan in the Madhouse*, it was part of a week of programmes about the singer broadcast in September 2005. Before the fifty-minute film was made, the producers had asked for anyone who remembered watching the original play to contact them, or better still anyone who had recorded it.

The original broadcast was a decade before domestic video-recording of course, so the only chance of anyone having a visual record would have to be a techno tele-buff with access to some highly specialised equipment, or someone who actually worked at the BBC and made an 'unofficial' copy before the master tape was wiped.

What the research did unearth were several sound recordings of varying quality, where early Dylan fans had taped Bob's songs straight from their television sets. These included 'Blowin' In The Wind', a strange song called 'Ballad Of The Gliding Swan', and a couple of other songs that would never appear in later Dylan recordings. But unfortunately, no video holy grail was uncovered, so the programme makers had to make do with interviews with *Madhouse* director Philip Saville, actor David Warner, writer Evan Davies and so on, plus singers who remembered a very young-looking Bob Dylan appearing at folk venues during that first, very low-key sojourn in London.

THE SIXTH STONE

LONDON, 1963

Similar to Stuart Sutcliffe, the 'fifth Beatle' who left the group
before they became famous, there was also a 'sixth Stone',
though he actually remained working with the Rolling Stones
right up to his death in 1985.

His name was Ian Stewart, a pianist who was playing with
Brian Jones in 1962 when they met up with Mick Jagger and
Keith Richards. The foursome were short of a bass player and
drummer, but once they recruited Bill Wyman and Charlie
Watts respectively, the six-piece Stones were ready to roll.

As they started to make a name for themselves on the
fledgling R & B circuit around London in 1963, the group
came to the notice of Andrew Loog Oldham, a PR guy working
with the Beatles, who were by then the biggest thing in British
pop. Oldham agreed to sign them to a management contract on
condition that they get rid of Stewart, because his face – literally
– didn't fit. Ian did have something of a 'lantern jaw' look, due
to a calcium deficiency when he was a child, but up till then his
powerful blues piano playing had been the most important
thing as far as the other Stones were concerned.

Now they had to choose between loyalty to Ian and possibly
to the band's future, so Ian had to go, though one suspects they
didn't all feel too good about it. Oldham, who later said he
suggested Stewart left simply because six was too big a group
for potential fans to remember the individuals, came up with a
compromise which they all agreed to – including Ian Stewart.
The pianist would act as the group's road manager, and play

piano where necessary on their records. When they finally made it big and toured the US in the mid-sixties, Ian was even known to play on stage behind a curtain from time to time.

'Stu', as the Stones always affectionately knew him, played on the group's records from their earliest singles right through to seventies and eighties hits like 'Angie', 'It's Only Rock 'n' Roll' and 'Start Me Up'. He died of a heart attack on 12 December 1985, still a friend and working colleague of the group who 'let him go' just when they were about to make it very, very big.

SPECTOR SCREWS SILL

LOS ANGELES, 1963

In 1961 the already-legendary producer Phil Spector formed a partnership with Lester Sill in Philles Records, the title an amalgam of their first names. Spector was developing his 'wall of sound' trademark style at the time, and soon had a string of massive hits on the label with the Ronettes, the Crystals and others. As the company's fortunes escalated, however, he noticeably began sidelining his partner, keeping him out of decision-making and so on.

A millionaire at 21, in 1962 Spector was being dubbed 'the Tycoon of Teen', his business acumen already much in evidence. When Sill agreed to sell his share of the company for $60,000, Spector refused to pay anything, claiming that Sill owed him money from the previous year. Sill reciprocated by suing his ex-partner, making a claim for the royalties of the next Crystals' record (at the time the label's biggest act) by way of compensation.

Early in 1963, Spector arranged a studio session with the Crystals, pianist Michael Spencer, a bass player and a drummer, to record a tune that he'd written specially for the occasion. Entitled '(Let's Dance) The Screw – Part 1', it had the girl group chanting incessantly 'C'mon and do . . . Dance the Screw . . .' with a chorus featuring nothing but the word 'dance' sung over and over. The whole thing was repeated several times, before they recorded a B-side '(Let's Dance) The Screw – Part 2' which consisted of virtually the same monotonous performance all over again. A few days later, a pressing of the single – the 'next Crystals' record' – landed in Lester Sill's mailbox, with a label stamped DJ COPY – NOT FOR SALE.

LENNON LASHES OUT

LIVERPOOL, 1963

Nineteen sixty-three was the year of British Beatlemania, when the 'Fab Four' topped the charts with four consecutive hits in their home country, prior to their conquering America and the rest of the world in 1964. Every move they made that year was followed by an eager media, happy to celebrate the country's new favourites, but as always on the lookout for any hint of scandal.

And Paul McCartney's 21st birthday party on 18 June 1963 was the scene of an incident that – had the tabloid press been as relentless in their pursuit of celebrity gossip as they are today – could have done the group's popularity far greater harm than it actually did.

The previous month, John Lennon had gone for a few days' holiday in Spain with the band's manager Brian Epstein. Given that Lennon was a married man with a two-month-old child, this was odd anyway – why didn't he take a break with his wife Cynthia? And Epstein was a known homosexual, which was still an illegal lifestyle back in 1963. Tongues, therefore, were bound to wag.

Things came to a head, however, at the McCartney birthday bash, held at an aunt's house in order to accommodate the many guests in a marquee erected in the garden. Bob Wooler, the local promoter and DJ at the Cavern Club who had helped the Beatles up the first rung of the ladder (before and after Epstein came into the picture), apparently made a remark to John Lennon about his recent trip to Spain.

The next second all hell broke loose as the Beatle attacked the hapless DJ so violently that the latter suffered a black eye, bruised ribs and torn knuckles (sustained from trying to protect his face as he was being kicked). According to the far-from-accurate biography *The Lives of John Lennon* by Albert Goldman, Wooler had jokingly said, 'How was the honeymoon, John?' In Ray Coleman's *John Winston Lennon*, Lennon's ex-wife Cynthia recalled, 'John said, "He called me a queer so I battered his bloody ribs in."' It was a violent side to Lennon that those close to him were not unfamiliar with, albeit brought on by drink on this occasion.

The next day, the *Daily Mirror* tabloid had picked up on the story, journalist Don Short quoting an apologetic Lennon (no doubt on a damage-limitation exercise instigated by Epstein) as saying, 'I was so high I didn't realise what I was doing.'

Luckily for Lennon, the injured Wooler was close enough to the Beatles and their manager to patch things up almost immediately. Had it been a virtual stranger that John had attacked at this pivotal point in the group's rise to fame, it's anybody's guess what effect the ensuing publicity (and possibly further 'revelations' about his Spanish sojourn with Epstein) might have had on their immediate career.

THE BOSS AT PRAYER

ASBURY PARK, NEW JERSEY, 1963

Bruce Springsteen, who grew up in a typical Italian-American household in New Jersey, was something of a handful if some of the stories are to be believed, like being smoked out of his room by his father for playing loud music. Bruce had a strict Catholic upbringing, but that didn't stop him being knocked over by a priest for being a bad altar boy and, at one stage, being stuffed in a garbage can by a nun!

But it was when Springsteen announced that he wanted to take up the guitar that his mother – who wanted him to be an author – was so concerned she sent him to the rectory to see the local priest, Father Ray.

'Hi, Father Ray, I'm Mr Springsteen's son,' he said. 'I got this problem. My father thinks I should be a lawyer, and my mother, she wants me to be an author. But I got this guitar.'

'This is too big a deal for me,' the Father replied. 'You gotta talk to God . . . tell him about the lawyer and the author . . .' before adding a note of caution: '. . . but don't say *nothin'* about that guitar!'

HOLY MODAL ROCKERS

NEW YORK CITY, 1963

For every rock group who have made it, there are hundreds who didn't, and some who didn't really have any ambition to. Yet in that last, determinedly 'uncommercial' bracket, there have been important artists who have exerted a huge influence without getting their names in lights. One such band, a catalyst from which sprang much of the New York 'underground' rock scene from the mid-sixties onwards, were the Holy Modal Rounders, formed in the early sixties by Peter Stampfel on banjo and fiddle, and Steve Weber on guitar.

Both had drifted onto the Greenwich Village scene from Wisconsin and Philadelphia respectively and from the start they represented an anarchic approach to musicianship, rehearsal and performance that wasn't going to change as the band progressed (if that was the right word). With an eclectic repertoire that took in songs from the twenties, thirties or whenever, with changed lyrics here and altered tunes there, they then delivered the result in an often chaotic mix of bluegrass, blues and pre-rock pop styles, a 'progressive old-time' sound that defied accurate categorisation.

However, what united Stampfel and Weber from the start was their common love of traditional folk styles. Stampfel, born in 1938, grew up in a musical environment that included bluegrass, blues and of course fifties rock 'n' roll. But, like many of his generation, disillusioned with what they felt was real rock's demise in the late fifties, he'd caught the beatnik bug and so (apparently following a girl he'd met in San Francisco) made it to New York, specifically the East Village.

Interviewed by Billy Bob Harguss in 1996, he gives an insight into how, by the late fifties, the 'Village' was a Mecca for itinerant youth such as he. 'The competition was who had the cheapest place. This one guy had a place on Fifth Street between B and C in a basement for $15 a week! In '59, I was aware that the East Village was hip and the West Village was square. The East Village had the coolest people. The people living in the Village proper were more likely to be phoneys. It was ridiculous stuff! Young people are always preoccupied with being "hipper than thou", t'was ever thus.'

After four or so years around the folk scene with a variety of short-lived groups, Stampfel met Weber, whom he was to describe as, 'the long lost kid brother I never even thought I had'. Before they met, Weber's reputation went before him, most of it dubious to say the least. Apparently a street-dwelling speed freak that picked his all-black clothes out of garbage cans, Stampfel expected him to be a no-hoper folkie, not a brilliant blues guitarist.

Immediately they met in 1963, they formed what would eventually become the Holy Modal Rounders after a succession of name changes. 'First they were the Total Quintessence Stomach Pumpers,' Stampfel would recall, 'then the Temporal Worth High Steppers and then the Motherfucker Creek Babyrapers. That was just a joke name. He was Rinky-Dink Steve the Tin Horn and I was Fast Lightning Cumquat. He was Teddy Boy Forever and I was Wild Blue Yonder. It kept changing names. Then it was the Total Modal Rounders. Then when we were stoned on pot someone else, Steve Close maybe, said Holy Modal Rounders by mistake.' And by common consent of their growing coterie of fans around the Village, that was the name that stuck.

Steve Weber's general working style was unprofessional in the extreme; he was reluctant to rehearse, sometimes even to get out of bed, so gigs were therefore often a hit-and-miss affair. Yet despite this unreliability, the duo managed to make two albums on the Prestige label in 1964 (*Holy Modal Rounders* and

II), both in the quirky-folk mould that by then had made them a cult attraction in New York, with Stampfel's left-field approach to songwriting very much in evidence. He described his writing style back then to Richie Unterberger in the latter's 1998 book *Unknown Legends Of Rock 'n' Roll*: 'When I started writing songs, I wasn't very good. I mostly did it the way Bob Dylan started writing songs in 1961, which was putting new words to old songs. Which, of course, is what Woody Guthrie did a lot before Dylan.'

They went on to move in a more acid-rock direction when they hit the studio again in 1967, this time with the future playwright and actor Sam Shepard on drums. The resulting album, *Indian War Hoop*, was on the highly progressive ESP label, as was *The Moray Eels Eat the Holy Modal Rounders*, which appeared the following year, now considered by many a classic of deranged psychedelia, which gelled country, blues, ragtime and general musical mayhem into a sometimes incomprehensible whole. Compared favourably by some with the Mothers of Invention's *We're Only in It for the Money*, the album featured the one song – 'Bird Song' – that put the Rounders music in front of a far broader audience, when it was used in 1969 on the soundtrack of the seminal acid-road movie *Easy Rider*.

Highly influential in the impact they made on those around them, Weber's lack of 'professional' ambition and both his and Stampfel's musical integrity meant the band would never achieve commercial success, but their story ranks them among the great unsung heroes of rock 'n' roll.

THE STONES WERE A COVERS BAND

LONDON, 1963–4

Although the songwriting team of Mick Jagger and Keith Richards has been responsible for most of the Rolling Stones' many hits, the group actually launched their success in the singles charts with a series of cover versions.

After their debut with Chuck Berry's 'Come On' (which only made Number 21 in the UK) in July 1963, followed by the Beatles' 'I Wanna Be Your Man' (Number Twelve, November 1963, though not actually a cover at the time), they made Number Three in February 1964 with Buddy Holly's 'Not Fade Away'. Then followed their first two UK chart-toppers: 'It's All Over Now', originally recorded by the Valentinos, and Willie Dixon's 'Little Red Rooster' (in July and November 1964 respectively). And their first Top Twenty entry in America was in November 1964 with 'Time Is On My Side', previously an R & B hit for Irma Thomas. It was a full twenty months from the Stones' chart debut before they made it big with an original – 'The Last Time' in March 1965.

JOHN PEEL'S DAYS AS A BEATLES BUFF

TEXAS, 1964

The highly influential British DJ and radio presenter John Peel, who died in 2004, was regarded as something of a national institution – yet he started his career in broadcasting as a 'token Liverpudlian' on a Texas radio station in an early-sixties America besotted by the Beatles.

Born in 1939 in Heswall, a Cheshire town not far from Liverpool, John Robert Parker Ravenscroft was the son of an upper-middle-class cotton merchant. After finishing his then-compulsory National Service in the army in 1959 – in the Royal Artillery as a B2 Radar Operator – he briefly worked as a mill operative in Rochdale before heading for the United States, home of the rock 'n' roll he was already obsessed with.

John got a job with a cotton producer who dealt with his father and for nearly a year he worked in the Dallas Cotton Exchange, progressing to selling crop insurance in west Texas. It was also in Dallas that he got to speak to John F Kennedy during his 1960 election campaign and, following Kennedy's assassination in the city in 1963, he bluffed his way into the midnight press conference at which Lee Harvey Oswald was charged with the murder, by claiming to be a reporter for the *Liverpool Echo*. It was shortly before Oswald's assassination, so later on he did actually phone in a story to the Merseyside newspaper.

It was while John was in Dallas that he got his first radio job, albeit unpaid, working for WRR Radio where he presented the second hour of a Monday night programme *Kat's Karavan*. However, it was when Beatlemania hit the States in the early months of 1964 that he began to make his mark, when another Dallas station, KLIF, took him on as their 'official' Beatles correspondent. This was partly on account of his 'Liverpool' accent, which despite his posh boarding-school background, he soon hammed up to his advantage.

'I became a Beatles expert, but of course I hadn't been in Liverpool for years and didn't know anything about them,' Peel would recall years later: 'In those days, though, America was full of DJs who were all called James Bond who pretended to be English and were really Canadian and who were all Ringo's cousin. I don't know why they chose Ringo. So, in the sense that I wasn't called James Bond and I really did come from England, I was almost unique.'

A year later, John moved to Oklahoma City to join one of the city's radio stations, KOMA, where he spent the next eighteen months, and it was here that he underwent his first name change, dropping the 's' from his surname and broadcasting as John Ravencroft. At KOMA he was paired up with a comedy jock on the breakfast show, but his northern wit was lost on his co-presenter and he was soon shunted off to an evening slot before eventually being 'let go' by the station.

His next stop was California and it was there, at KMEN radio in San Bernardino, that he really started to flex his musical muscles. In Dallas and Oklahoma John had reluctantly stuck to the playlist, playing popular tracks for screaming teeny-boppers and Beatles fans. But at KMEN he began to act like the broadcaster that British audiences would become familiar with, playing pretty much whatever he liked. San Bernardino's location helped too; John was only sixty miles east of Los Angeles – an ideal location for checking out gigs and hanging out with bands. It was 1965, and through the next year or so Peel witnessed the first stirrings of Flower Power at first hand; he was right there in the middle of it all, where the 'psychedelic' revolution was taking place. 'I went off to work in California where I started taking drugs and leading a generally depraved kind of life,' was how the DJ would sardonically describe his move to the West Coast.

'I started to play records that I wanted to play,' Peel said of his days at KMEN. 'Previously it had been all chart stuff. But I had to do six hours over the weekend and I thought, if I was going to do six hours, then I'm going to play what I want to play. I started to play blues things, Doors, Love, Butterfield Blues Band and Jefferson Airplane. I worked there for eighteen months and then ran foul of the law and thought I'd better leave.'

Legend has it that the local sheriff in San Bernardino had it in for KMEN and its radical 'hippy' DJs, so, fearing arrest and possible deportation, John booked a flight under his middle names and flew back to the UK. It was after joining the new offshore 'pirate' station, Radio London, to present the midnight-to-two slot (that developed into a programme called *The Perfumed Garden*) that he first adopted the name John Peel, leaving his American career as a 'professional Liverpudlian' behind him forever.

PAUL'S BABY

LIVERPOOL, 1964

Girlfriends, fans, groupies and other hangers-on always surrounded the Beatles from the earliest days they played the cellar clubs of Liverpool and Hamburg. So it was almost inevitable that rumours of illegitimate children, paternity cases and even abortion would follow in the wake of their progress, and over the years the number of 'claims' concerning Beatle-fathered pregnancies meant the band would have had to spend all their time having sex had every one been genuine.

In Paul McCartney's case, however, at least two substantial-sounding claims to his fathering a child were made, one of which has never been denied. First there was the child born to the daughter of one of the club owners in Hamburg's Grosse Freiheit Strasse where the Beatles played in the early sixties.

The mother, Erika Hubers, was a pretty girl with long, straight hair; she had been working as a waitress in one of her father's clubs when Paul had allegedly dated her during one of the Beatles' final seasons in the German port. Erika claimed that Paul had known she was pregnant and encouraged her to have an abortion, but she refused and a daughter, Bettina, was born the day the group left Hamburg. Some time later, just when the Beatles were making it as the biggest thing in pop, legal documents were drawn up by Erika's father's solicitors in Germany and delivered to the law firm acting for Brian Epstein and the group. Paul denied any responsibility and the documents were returned to Hamburg unanswered, the Beatles' legal eagles working on the assumption that a long-drawn-out passage of the case through the German courts would cause less of a stir than if the matter came to a head in the glare of publicity it would attract in the UK.

That wasn't good enough for Erika's family however, and after they threatened once more to file papers in the English courts a settlement was reached in 1966. Then, in 1981, clearly with an eye on the money her alleged 'father' was worth, Bettina Hubers – now an adult – resumed the action in the courts, with Paul McCartney continuing to deny his paternity.

A potentially more damaging threat to the Beatle's image came with a paternity claim made in Liverpool early in 1964. A local girl had given birth to a baby boy, citing Paul McCartney as the father. Again Paul denied everything, but a meeting was arranged between the girl, her mother and an associate of the Beatles' lawyers in Liverpool. The lawyer reported back that all the girl seemed to want was some modest payment towards the cost of a pram for the baby, and recommended this should be paid before the matter developed any further.

While this was being arranged, however, the girl's mother mentioned the matter to a friend (some subsequent rumours claimed it was a close relative) who pointed out how much the child could really be claiming. The next development was the most explosive of all as far as Epstein and the Beatles were concerned. As fans queued up outside a Liverpool cinema to greet the group at the premiere of their film *A Hard Day's Night*, early in July 1964, leaflets were circulated by a member of the girl's family outlining her plight. This was later on the same day that the group had been welcomed back to their home town with a civic reception hosted by the Mayor at the Town Hall. Any scandal couldn't have come at a worse moment.

Epstein and his legal advisors went into full damage-limitation mode, drawing up an agreement that stipulated a four-figure payment to the girl (a not inconsiderable sum in 1964) on the condition that Paul would continue to deny being the father of the child, and that the payment didn't in any way represent an admission. Also, in the eventuality of a court action that proved to the satisfaction of the court that the child was indeed Paul McCartney's, the maximum payment the court could order for the maintenance and education of the child was two pounds ten shillings (£2.50) a week until he was 21. In consideration for the money paid to her, the girl agreed never to make any claim against McCartney in the future or allege that he was the father or disclose the terms of the agreement; otherwise she would be liable to return the payment.

Luckily for the Beatles the whole affair was thus damped down, and the 'paternity' leaflets were just brushed off by the press as another crank trying make a killing at the group's expense; by the middle of 1964, there were plenty of them about.

There was one postscript to the case however. Some years later the affair was dragged up in a British tabloid newspaper, revealing the identity of a Liverpool man who was 'Beatle Paul's love child' – his name, too, was Paul.

LEADER OF THE PACK

NEW YORK CITY, 1964

The legendary producer George 'Shadow' Morton, who created a series of teen angst classics with the Shangri Las, came up with their biggest ever hit literally off the top of his head.

After penning the four-piece girl group's first huge smash 'Remember (Walkin' In The Sand)' in 1964, he was signed to a songwriting contract by the team of Jerry Leiber and Mike Stoller, who at the time were running the Red Bird label that released all the Shangri Las' material.

One day Morton was confronted by Leiber, asking if he had a song as a follow-up to 'Remember'.

'He says, "Do you have anything? Because if you don't, I'm gonna get Jeff and Ellie to start working on something,"' Morton recalled. Jeff Barry and Ellie Greenwich were among the top songwriters working closely with Leiber and Stoller.

'When I heard that I said, "I got a song." He said, "What's it about?"

'I was up on 11th Avenue that morning, looking at motorcycles. So I said, "It's about . . . a motorcycle!"

'He said, "A motorcycle? What about a motorcycle?"

'I said, "It's . . . about this guy who rides a motorcycle. The whole story is really about this guy – and he rides a motorcycle into this little town . . . and this girl sees him, and she falls in love with him."'

Leiber felt the idea was a little lightweight, to say the least. 'Is that it? It doesn't sound right to me. You're talking about a

Hell's Angels-type guy driving into town and falling in love with this little girl. I don't think it's a good idea. DJs aren't gonna play that.'

But Morton persisted with his improvisation about a song that had actually yet to be written, insisting, 'It gets better . . .'

'It gets better, how does it get better?'

'He dies.'

The resulting record, eventually written with the aid of Barry and Greenwich, was 'Leader Of The Pack', which shot to the top of the charts and became the Shangri Las' greatest-ever hit, and has been the anthem icon of motorcycle rock ever since.

DEATH IN A MOTEL

LOS ANGELES, 1964

In the early hours of 11 December 1964, soul superstar Sam Cooke was shot dead 'in self defence' by the lady manager of a cheap motel in the run-down Watts district of Los Angeles. The circumstances leading up to the shooting also involved Cooke in the alleged attempted rape of another woman, though that was never proven. What is true is that the death of one of rock's true pioneers could have come about by a mistaken assumption on the part of his slayer.

Sam Cooke had been having dinner with friends, Al Schmitt and his wife Joan, at a smart Italian restaurant, Martoni's, when he was introduced to Elisa Boyer by a PR man from his record company. He left the Martoni in the company of Boyer, having arranged to meet the Schmitts at PJ's, a nightclub on Sunset Boulevard, at around 1 a.m. By 1.30 a.m., the Schmitts had tired of waiting for Sam, leaving the bar to drive home. Sam and Elisa arrived at PJ's not long after that, perhaps missing the Schmitts by just a few minutes. Boyer would later recall that there was some kind of tension between Sam and a man who'd started chatting to her while Cooke was talking to some other friends. That was when they decided to leave.

According to Boyer, when she asked Cooke to take her home, he drove his red Ferrari down to the Watts district instead, where he checked into a $3-a-night room at the Hacienda Motel, signing in under his own name. This in itself was odd, as the Schmitts would testify that the singer had been flashing a wad of $100 bills just earlier in the evening. At this stage, Boyer claimed, she had in effect been kidnapped by Cooke, who 'dragged' her up to the room. That wasn't particularly evident to 55-year-old Bertha Franklin, the motel manager who booked them in, who recalled that Boyer 'didn't say a word' when they were in her office checking in.

As to what happened next, behind the closed door of the motel room, there was only Boyer's version of events to rely on. According to the woman, she once more pleaded to be taken home, whereupon Cooke threw her on the bed and, in her words, 'pulled my sweater off and ripped my dress . . . I knew he was going to rape me.' When Cooke allowed her to go to the bathroom she tried to get out of the window but it was locked, but she then managed to slip out of the bedroom, picking up her clothes and handbag – and most of Sam's clothes – as she fled. Dressed only in a slip and bra, she apparently went down to the manager's office and knocked on the door, but Franklin was on the phone in her apartment behind the office and by the time she opened the door Boyer was gone. Outside in the street, the fleeing woman pulled on her sweater and skirt, dumped Cooke's clothes (which she would explain she'd taken to stop him following her) under a nearby stairwell, and then rang the police from a phone booth.

Meanwhile, back at the Hacienda, there was another knock on Bertha Franklin's door; this time it was Sam Cooke, dressed only in an overcoat and shoes and demanding, 'Where's the girl?' When Franklin said she had no idea, Cooke went outside and started to drive off in his car, when he had what proved to be a fatal change of mind. He pulled up outside the office, having suddenly decided that Boyer was probably hiding in Franklin's apartment.

'He just kept saying where was the girl,' Franklin recalled later. 'I told him to get the police if he wanted to search my place. He said, "Damn the police," and started working on the door with his shoulder . . . It wasn't long before he was in . . . When he walked in, he walked straight to the kitchen, and then he came back and went into the bedroom. Then he came out. I was standing there on the floor and he grabbed both of my arms and started twisting them and asking me where was the girl.' Unknown to Sam, the motel's owner Evelyn Carr, who Franklin had been talking to, was able to hear all of this over the open phone line.

The two got into a tussle, with Franklin scratching and biting the star, who only got angrier as a result. Pushing Cooke away, the manager grabbed a .22-calibre handgun that she kept on the TV set in case of hold-ups. She fired three shots, almost at point-blank range, two of which nevertheless missed. The third, fired with the muzzle less than two inches from Sam, entered the left side of his chest, passed through his left lung, then his heart, and then his right lung.

As Sam staggered across the room bleeding profusely and mumbling, 'Lady, you shot me,' Franklin – not realising the singer was already fatally wounded – started battering him over the head with a broomstick. 'The first time I hit him, it broke . . . It was very flimsy.' Sam Cooke collapsed to the floor, falling against the broken door jamb. He was dead.

At about the same time that Cooke was trying to break into Franklin's room, Elisa Boyer was in a phone booth waiting for the police, who she'd phoned, reporting that she'd been kidnapped – they'd told her to stay right there. While Boyer awaited their arrival, police headquarters got another call, this time from Evelyn Carr who said she'd heard what sounded like a break-in at the motel, followed by gunshots.

Officer Wallace Cook was first on the scene. By 4 a.m. the apartment was photographed, evidence seized and Sam Cooke's body taken to the morgue. The case was then handed over to Los Angeles Police Detectives Fred Thomas and Douglas Kesler.

A coroner's inquest was held on 16 December 1964, at which Franklin and Boyer repeated their stories. A medical examiner testified that in addition to the fatal bullet wound and the lump on his head, Sam had a few small scratches on his left cheek and forehead. And a police officer reported that although the singer's credit cards were missing, a money clip with $108 was found in his overcoat pocket. After just fifteen minutes of deliberation, the seven-member coroner's jury ruled the shooting was 'justifiable homicide' and the case was closed.

However, on 11 January 1965, exactly one month after the shooting, Elisa Boyer was arrested in Hollywood for prostitution. That gives a clue to a far more likely scenario than the one she told the police about Cooke. In the first place, why would a high roller like Sam Cooke choose a cheap motel if he was hoping to seduce his pick-up? It also transpired that the Hacienda was known as a hooker's hang-out. Prostitutes have commonly been known to steal a customer's clothes to steal any money or valuables in the pockets and to prevent the owner giving chase. That could be why Cooke was demanding to know where Boyer was, thinking Franklin was in on the scam.

One question posed by the prostitution theory is why would Boyer have run to Franklin's office if she had just rolled a customer? It's possible she thought she could hide there for a few minutes by telling Franklin, falsely, that she'd been attacked. Or indeed Franklin may have been a party to the whole thing. We'll never know, but what the music world did know, as soon as the news broke of Sam Cooke's death, was that it had lost one of its true original voices in an incident that has never been fully explained.

FIGHTIN' TALK

LONDON, 1964

When Bob Dylan's third album *The Times They Are A-Changin'* was released in 1964, the Irish folk singer Dominic Behan was incensed to find that the young American was cited as the sole composer of 'With God on Our Side', the tune of which Behan claimed to have written himself some time before as 'The Patriot Game'. But as was the case with many folk singers and folk songs, it was a fairly common occurrence for a new adaptation to appear of a traditional song, the updated version being credited to that particular singer, and Behan's version had likewise evolved from an earlier source.

According to Liam Clancy of famed folk-duo the Clancy Brothers, 'The Patriot Game' was written by Dominic Behan but was originally a song from the Appalachian mountains called 'The Merry Month Of May'. It had then become more popular when it was adapted by a singer called Joe Stafford, who named it 'The Bold Grenadier', and it was from that recording that Dominic Behan took the tune that became 'The Patriot Game'.

Clancy would recall how they would sing the Behan song around the folk clubs of Greenwich Village, where their audience often included the young Bob Dylan, who eventually appropriated the tune for 'With God On Our Side.'

But initially that didn't stop Behan, twelve years Dylan's senior, chiding him publicly and, so legend has it, contacting the star in his hotel suite during one of his early British tours. Apparently Dylan picked up the phone, and upon hearing

Behan's uncompromising tirade, attempted to calm the conversation down. 'My lawyers can speak with your lawyers' – or words to that effect – didn't placate the angry Irishman however, whose alleged reply was, 'I've got two lawyers, and they're on the end of my wrists!'

THE BEATLES AT BUCKINGHAM PALACE

LONDON, 1965

Soon after the Beatles went to Buckingham Palace to be presented with their MBEs (Member of the British Empire) in October 1965, John Lennon claimed they had shared a quick joint in a royal bathroom prior to being greeted by the Queen. The story spread like wildfire of course and was accepted as being true at the time. Only when George and Paul denied it some time later – McCartney remembered simply having a 'sly ciggy' with the other three in order to calm their nerves – did it come into question. Ringo, perhaps only fuelling the rumour, claimed he couldn't remember one way or the other. Lennon, however, later insisted he'd made the whole thing up, adding, 'We'd have been far too scared to do it.'

John Lennon, of course, famously returned his MBE in 1969 when he had his chauffeur deliver the decoration back to Buckingham Palace. An accompanying letter to Queen Elizabeth II read: 'I am returning this MBE in protest against Britain's involvement in the Nigeria–Biafra thing, against our support of America in Vietnam, and against "Cold Turkey" slipping down the charts. With love, John Lennon of Bag.' The 'Nigeria–Biafra thing' referred to a conflict going on at the time in Africa, and 'Cold Turkey' was a single he'd made with the Plastic Ono Band and produced with Yoko Ono as 'Bag Productions'.

WHEN THE BEATLES MET ELVIS

LOS ANGELES, 1965

John Lennon had been famously quoted as saying that, 'before Elvis there was nothing'. The other three Beatles all shared his regard for the rock 'n' roll originator whom they had idolised as teenagers and from whom they drew their primary inspiration.

But by 1965, the Liverpool quartet had assumed the position that Elvis had occupied the previous decade, as the most famous and influential rock artists on the planet. It was with some trepidation therefore, that both parties agreed to a meeting, arranged almost with the secrecy of a military operation by their respective managements.

Almost any journalist in the world would have jumped at the chance to have covered the occasion, but both camps were so nervous of something 'going wrong', guests and host not hitting it off, that all but one – who was not allowed to make any notes – were barred.

The arrangement was for the Beatles to visit their old hero in his Bel Air home in Los Angeles. Getting there involved two black limousines: one was carrying Brian Epstein, Elvis's manager Colonel Tom Parker and the sole newspaperman Chris Hutchins (one of the few journalists who was 'well in' with both managers); the other, riding in convoy, contained all four Beatles and their two assistants, Mal Evans and Neil Aspinall.

As both cars left the gates of the mansion in Benedict Canyon where the Liverpudlians were staying, police motor-cycle riders pulled into the road behind them to prevent anyone following. Police cars blocked the roadway, holding up traffic as the limos sped along Sunset Boulevard before the road turned up out of Beverly Hills to Bel Air where Elvis had his home at 565 Perugia Way.

The only first-hand account of the legendary meeting came from writer Hutchins who, though told not to make notes, did so by slipping out to the bathroom every so often. Hutchins's record of the evening confirmed what everyone feared – there were going to be as many awkward silences as genial banter, and a certain amount of friction as well.

When the party arrived at the Presley home, Elvis and Priscilla – not yet married – were sitting in the King's den. Hutchins would record that Elvis was wearing 'a red shirt and close-fitting black jerkin, the high Napoleonic collar rising above his sideburns', while his bride-to-be was 'pure Hollywood starlet' with black bouffant hair, eyes thick with mascara and midnight-blue eyeliner, 'wearing a figure-hugging, sequinned mini-dress, black seamed stockings and black high heels'.

Elvis was surrounded by his usual 'Memphis Mafia' entourage of minders, whose wives and children were gathered in the adjoining games room. Priscilla went to join 'the girls' as Elvis greeted his guests, seemingly relaxed but probably as nervous as they were.

John Lennon tried to break the ice with a Peter Sellers 'Inspector Clouseau' voice – 'Oh, zere you are' – but Elvis just looked bemused as he sat down with John and Paul on his right, and Ringo and George on his left. This was embarrassing for all concerned, as no one knew what to say next. Finally Elvis broke the silence, saying that if the Englishmen were just going to sit and stare at him, he'd be going to bed – or would they prefer to jam a little?

Always the diplomat, Paul agreed that was a good idea and guitars were brought in and plugged into amps, Elvis picking up the bass guitar, John and George two rhythm guitars and Paul sitting at a white piano that had been wheeled into view. Elvis apologised to Ringo for there being no drum kit, 'We left that back in Memphis,' but the drummer assured him he'd rather play pool.

Things got a little more relaxed as they tuned up and started to strum some chords, Paul quipping, 'Elvis, lad, you're coming along quite well. Keep up the rehearsals and me and Mr Epstein will make you a star.' They swapped stories about scary plane journeys, over-the-top fans rushing the stage, that kind of thing. Suddenly it was apparent they actually had a lot in common, as Elvis asked, 'What's it gonna be?'

The twenty or so people in the company of Elvis and the Beatles that night were about to witness the most valuable line-up in pop history give its one and only performance. 'Let's do one by the other Cilla – Cilla Black,' McCartney suggested, leading into 'You're My World'.

Elvis's rich voice came over as far more powerful than the others', as his left leg moved up and down in time to the beat, and he was joined by Paul on some vocal choruses. George Harrison worked in some typically tight little riffs while John – whom Hutchins felt was going through the motions to a degree – played with his usual assured confidence.

One number segued into another before John rattled Elvis a little by asking him why he wasn't playing any rock 'n' roll, any more. Elvis, one of the inventors of rock 'n' roll, was quick to reply, saying that just because he was embroiled in movies didn't mean he couldn't rock any more: 'I might just get around to cuttin' a few sides and knockin' you off the top.'

Things slowly but surely went downhill from then on, as far as Lennon's relationship with his former idol was concerned. Seeing a model of a covered wagon carrying the slogan 'All the Way With LBJ' (LBJ being President Johnson, who Lennon saw as being guilty of perpetuating the war in Vietnam), the Beatle continued to rile Presley with barbed comments about his movie-making, to the point where the host called over to two of his 'Mafia' minders that 'that sonovabitch' was 'stoned out of his mind'.

Brian Epstein intervened to make sure that the bad feeling didn't escalate further, but even as the party broke up at 2 a.m., Lennon couldn't resist one final jibe in his cod-French accent: 'Sanks for ze music, Elvis. Long live ze King!'

After the evening with Elvis, Lennon's public account of the meeting was effusive: 'There's only one person in the United States of America that we ever wanted to meet – not that he wanted to meet us! And we met him last night . . . We can't tell you how we felt. We just idolised him so much. The only person we wanted to meet in the USA was Elvis Presley. We can't tell you what a thrill that was.' Privately John would tell friends, 'It was just like meeting Engelbert Humperdink.'

Elvis later put out a press statement regarding the Beatles that ended with, 'They are entertainers like myself and I guess they're as dedicated as the rest of us. Which, in the long run, is all that matters. I wish them luck.' Reading it, Lennon retorted to Chris Hutchins, 'I'm not sure who's the bigger bullshitter – him or me.'

THE MAN WHO TURNED DOWN 'YESTERDAY'

LONDON, 1965

The story of the Beatles is littered with 'if onlys' – chances missed by various individuals in relation to the group's phenomenal conquest of the world of pop music through the sixties.

Most famous of all was Dick Rowe of Decca Records, who dismissed them with the comment that there was no future in guitar groups. And their first 'manager', local Liverpool entrepreneur Allan Williams, would dine out for years on the fact that he was 'the man who gave the Beatles away', referring to Brian Epstein signing the band after they had apparently reneged on their quasi-formal arrangement with him. Likewise, there were scores of concert promoters and club owners across Britain who turned down the chance of booking the band just prior to their rise to the top in the early months of 1963.

But one of the lesser-known examples of somebody kicking themselves for missing a Fab Four chance was in 1965, when singer Billy J Kramer, a fellow member of the Epstein stable of Liverpool acts, was looking for a song for his new single.

Billy J approached Paul McCartney (whom he'd known since the days they were all unknowns together on Merseyside), asking if he'd written anything new he could use. Kramer had already scored with hits from the pen of Lennon and McCartney, starting with his debut 'Do You Want To Know A Secret' (a chart Number Two), followed by the chart-topping 'Bad to Me' and 'I'll Keep You Satisfied' (Number Four), all

103

in 1963. He'd made the Top Ten again in 1964 with a number from the Beatle songsmith 'From A Window', so turning to McCartney to see if he had anything suitable was nothing new.

The Beatle played him a simple little ballad that he'd recently written on the guitar, nothing fancy, just a plaintive song perhaps a little too wistful to be a chart-smashing single. For whatever reason, Kramer didn't think it was strong enough and turned it down.

That song was 'Yesterday' and by the end of the decade over a thousand recording artists worldwide – from Ray Charles to Frank Sinatra, Willie Nelson to Diana Ross – had covered it; even Elvis would have it as part of his live repertoire in Las Vegas. 'Yesterday' was simply the most successful song to appear under the Lennon–McCartney credit line, although it was entirely Paul's creation; on McCartney's own version, it was the first song to be recorded by just one of the Fab Four without the other three taking part.

Billy J did score again, with a version of Burt Bacharach's 'Trains And Boats And Planes', which made Number Twelve in the UK charts in mid-1965, but one wonders whether the magic of 'Yesterday' would have worked for him too if he'd not passed on it.

WHO KILLED BOBBY FULLER?

LOS ANGELES, 1966

Bobby Fuller was a singer and guitarist who had one big hit in the mid-sixties as leader of the Bobby Fuller Four, and a burgeoning reputation cut short by a 'suicide' that remains one of the great mysteries of rock 'n' roll.

Fuller was born in Baytown, Texas, in 1942; his idol was Buddy Holly, who had died in the fatal plane crash in February 1959 that also claimed the Big Bopper and Richie Valens. Initially modelling his music on Holly and his group the Crickets, Fuller formed his Four in the early sixties, moving from Texas to LA in 1964 when they were signed to Del-Fi Records, the label that had represented Richie Valens.

Although Bobby was himself an excellent songwriter, the Bobby Fuller Four's third release, which catapulted them into the charts, was a cover of an old Crickets number, 'I Fought The Law'. It was released in October 1965, and by January 1966 was in the national Top Ten in *Billboard* magazine, the single also enjoying a modest showing at Number 33 in the UK charts. Del-Fi didn't have much faith in Fuller's songwriting it seems, so the Four's next releases were also covers; but when none of these followed in the footsteps of 'I Fought The Law' things began to fall apart within the group.

After a long and stressful tour in the summer of 1966, with the band on the verge of breaking up, Bobby returned to LA that July to start putting together his next recording project with a new line-up of musicians. One of his original band members, guitarist Jim Reese, had just been drafted to Vietnam and was going to sell his Jaguar XKE to Bobby; they'd arranged to meet the next day, 18 July, when Bobby also had a meeting scheduled at Del-Fi Records.

But Bobby never made the record-company meeting, nor the one with Reese to clinch the car deal. Wondering what was happening, at around 5 p.m. the band went to Bobby's apartment to see if he was there. His car wasn't in the parking lot and there was no one at his home. Bobby's mother, who was visiting from El Paso, had gone out briefly and when she returned she noticed that her son's car was back in the lot. Opening the door on the driver's side, she was immediately taken aback by the strong smell of petrol. Seeing Bobby lying in the front seat, with the keys in the ignition and his hand on the keys, she at first thought he was asleep, but after calling his name and getting no response, she realised that he was dead. He was 23 years old.

The official Los Angeles County Coroner's Office autopsy report read: 'Deceased was found lying face down in front seat of car – a gas can, one-third full, cover open – windows were all rolled up & doors shut, not locked – keys not in ignition.' The report, which also mentioned excessive bruising on his chest and shoulders, attributed the cause of death to asphyxiation, 'due to inhalation of gasoline'. Bobby was drenched in the fuel – some of which he'd also swallowed – his clothes and hair saturated; his body was found in a full state of rigor mortis, a clear indication that he'd been dead for over three hours. Furthermore, eyewitnesses testified that Bobby looked battered, as though he'd been in a fight, and that 'his right index finger was broken, as if it had been bent back'. Incredibly, in the face of all the facts pointing to the contrary, the Los Angeles Police Department concluded Bobby's death was a suicide, their official report stating, 'there was no evidence of foul play'.

Exactly what happened before the car returned (with or without Bobby at the wheel) has remained a mystery, but he was definitely in the apartment in the early morning hours of 18 July. Both his mother and the band's roadie (who was staying there) confirm that between midnight and 1 a.m. Bobby was there, watching TV and talking on the phone. According to the roadie, at around 1 or 2 a.m. Bobby got a call and left, and didn't come back. The last person to report seeing Bobby alive was Lloyd Esinger, the manager of the apartment complex. Apparently the singer, whom Esinger said appeared to be in good spirits, had stopped by his apartment at around 3 a.m. that night, and they had a few beers.

After his death, rumours began to circulate of Bobby having gone to an LSD party and dying there in a fall, and the people at the party having tried to make it look like a suicide to avert attention from themselves. But what really happened would seem to involve more sinister aspects.

It seems that an insurance policy had been taken out on Bobby Fuller's life for between $800,000 and $1 million, payable in the event of his death to a mysterious 'investor' in Del-Fi Records who was rumoured to have underworld connections. This was borne out by the arrival of three armed men at the apartment shared by Jim Reese and the Four's drummer Dalton Powell, just four days after Fuller's death – they were looking for Reese, who wasn't there when they turned up. Reese suspected it had something to do with an insurance policy taken out on his life: 'I had that insurance policy cancelled because I was worth a lot more dead to certain people, and I was taking no chances.'

Another possible angle involving the record company and their 'backers' was the fact that Del-Fi had profited handsomely seven years earlier when Ritchie Valens's death created an unnaturally high demand for his recordings. Contemplating their 'investment' starting to bomb commercially, certain people behind the scenes might have thought about the same turn of fortune happening again with Bobby Fuller.

Whatever the truth, it seems almost certain that someone was leaning on, or paying off, the notoriously corrupt LAPD. Besides the premature ruling of suicide, Bobby's brother Randy (who was bass player with the group) claims the cops never even checked the petrol can found in the car for prints, and when one of his uncles went down to the police station begging for an investigation, 'They told him if he knew what was good for him, he'd better keep his mouth shut.'

THE CHICAGO PLASTER CASTERS

CHICAGO, 1966

Cynthia Albritton was a nineteen-year-old art student whose tutor gave her a weekend assignment to make a plaster cast of 'something solid that could retain its shape'. It was 1966, and Cynthia was still a virgin; Paul Revere and the Raiders were playing in town along with British group the Hollies, so she and a girlfriend decided to get to meet the groups and, in her own words, 'maybe get laid'.

They succeeded on both counts, not least because she and her best friend had found the perfect gimmick, which immediately set them apart from all the other groupies. They formed 'The Plaster Casters of Chicago', and would persuade rock stars to drop their trousers by promising to immortalise their erect penises in plaster.

Although they never actually got to cast anyone on the Revere/Hollies date, their first casting conquest was spectacular in every way – Jimi Hendrix. By 1969 the Plaster Casters were so celebrated on the rock 'n' roll circuit – at least among musicians – that *Rolling Stone* magazine ran an article on them, and they even enjoyed the patronage of avant-garde rocker Frank Zappa (though he declined to be cast himself).

Cynthia – who is generally known as Cynthia Plaster Caster – and her partner Diana evolved a method of casting the rock stars' members in dental alginate and preserving the sculptures for posterity. As well as Hendrix, her rock celebrity casts include those of guitarist Harvey Mandel, the Lovin'

Spoonful's Zal Yanovsky and Led Zeppelin's notorious road manager Richard Cole.

As one writer observed, unlike most groupies Cynthia has more to show for her hard work than a possible quickie marriage and sticky divorce. Her celebrity plaster casts – which she affectionately refers to as her 'babies' – have been featured in several art exhibits and in 2002, *Plaster Caster*, a feature-length documentary on Cynthia's activities by filmmaker Jessica Villines was screened in film festivals throughout the United States.

Also in 2002, Cynthia founded the Cynthia P Caster Foundation, a legally sanctioned non-profit institution, whose mission is to help musicians and artists in financial need. The foundation raises its money through donations and the selling of limited edition art objects – including Cynthia's casts as well as her two-dimensional artwork.

THE BEATLES' NOTORIOUS 'BUTCHER' COVER

LOS ANGELES, 1966

In June 1966, a new Beatles album was released in the United States entitled *Yesterday and Today*, but when advance copies were sent out to DJs, radio stations and others, the recipients were shocked by what they saw.

Instead of the usual photos of four happy, smiling mop tops, the album's cover offered something quite different indeed: the Beatles, dressed in butchers' smocks, adorned with slabs of raw red meat, glass eyeballs, false teeth, and nude decapitated dolls, posing with what some saw as sick, sadistic leers on their faces. When those who'd received it began to complain about its gruesome sleeve, Capitol quickly withdrew the record. All promotional material for the album was destroyed, and it was reissued five days later with a substitute cover photo of the Beatles leaning on a steamer trunk. As every Beatle collector knows, many of the 750,000 or so original 'butcher' cover sleeves went back into record stores with a new cover pasted over the old one, and thousands of unwitting record buyers ended up purchasing albums whose covers could be peeled or steamed off to create what would become one of most sought-after pieces of Beatles memorabilia.

Over the years, the myth developed that the Beatles – tired of the way Capitol Records had been cutting up and rearranging their albums for the American market – deliberately planned the grotesque 'butcher cover' as a means of protesting at Capitol's 'butchery' of their records.

110

Nothing could have been further from the truth however; the photograph on the *Yesterday and Today* sleeve was not intended as the Beatles' protest against Capitol Records. In fact, not only was the 'butcher' photo never intended to be used as an album cover, it wasn't even the Beatles' idea. It was a single photograph from an earlier photo session, taken for entirely different reasons, before it was used, unfinished and out of context, for the sleeve of Capitol's new release.

The photo session that produced the notorious cover shot took place on 25 March 1966. Although the Beatles were certainly keen on the idea, and willing participants in the session that produced the bizarre photos, the man who actually came up with the concept behind the pictures was photographer Robert Whitaker. Whitaker, who ran a photographic studio in Melbourne, Australia, accompanied a journalist friend to an interview with Beatles manager Brian Epstein during the group's trip to Australia in June of 1964. Whitaker shot photos of Brian Epstein during the interview, and when the Beatles' manager saw the resulting prints, he was so impressed with the young photographer's work that he asked Whitaker to come and work for him. Whitaker accepted the job three months later, and he spent the next few years travelling with the Beatles and shooting them on their tours, in the recording studio, during private moments, and in arranged photo sessions. In fact Robert Whitaker was responsible for the 'steamer trunk' photo that replaced the butcher cover on *Yesterday and Today*, as well as the back cover of the *Revolver* album.

What, then, was the idea behind the photograph? As Whitaker would explain, the idea for the photo session came about because they 'were all really fed up at taking what one had hoped would be designer-friendly publicity pictures'. John Lennon, in an interview shortly before his death in 1980, echoed this view: 'It was inspired by our boredom and resentment at having to do "another" photo session and "another" Beatles thing. We were sick to death of it.' Whitaker had intended the session, of which the butcher photo was only one part, to be, 'his personal comment on the mass adulation of the group and the illusory nature of stardom'. As he later said, 'I had toured quite a lot of the world with them by then, and I was continually amused by the public adulation of four people . . .'

To that end, what he had planned was to form a triptych of pictures, something resembling a religious icon, to make the point that the Beatles were just as real and human as everyone else. The left-hand picture was of the Beatles facing a woman with her back to the camera, hanging on to a string of sausages. This picture was supposed to represent the 'birth' of the Beatles, with the sausages serving as an umbilical cord. The centre picture, the only one in colour, was the 'butcher' shot, and to its right there was one of George Harrison standing behind a seated John Lennon, hammer in hand, pounding nails into John's head. Whitaker explained that this picture was intended to demonstrate that the Beatles were not an illusion, not something to be worshipped, but people as real and substantial as 'a piece of wood'.

The 'butcher' picture itself was actually titled 'A Somnambulant Adventure', and its intention was to present a contrast, something shocking and completely out of line with the Beatles' public image. The one on the cover was unfinished, the final one was to have been against a gold background with silver jewelled halos around the boys' heads, offering a striking contrast between the Beatles' 'angelic' image and the gritty reality of the photograph. And it was never, ever, intended by either the photographer or the Beatles to end up as the cover on one of their albums.

BYRD REPLACED BY HORSE

CALIFORNIA, 1967

Rock stars, particularly those in groups rather than solo acts, are notoriously sensitive as to where they fit in the pecking order of things, the order of their names in credits and so on. Even the positioning of their image on an album can be a cause for concern – but no more so than with the Byrds in 1967, when David Crosby found his picture omitted altogether, its place being taken by a photograph of a horse!

The band had become mega stars in the States and worldwide, but personnel tensions were beginning to take their toll within the band. Roger McGuinn, Chris Hillman, Michael Clarke and David Crosby were starting work on their next album – which would eventually be *The Notorious Byrd Brothers* – when things finally came to a head. Clarke, the drummer, was dissatisfied with his status in the band, and left soon after, to be replaced by various session musicians.

David Crosby had been gradually assuming overall control of the way things were going in both the studio and on stage, with Hillman and McGuinn increasingly frustrated as a result. He'd caused friction with them at the Monterey Pop Festival by sitting in with Buffalo Springfield without even telling them and then, at the same event, he somewhat hijacked their own set by delivering a political tirade against the 'government cover-up' of the Kennedy assassination, which the others found totally embarrassing.

Tensions really came to a head when Crosby told Hillman and McGuinn he wasn't going to record a song written by

113

Gerry Goffin and Carole King because it would mean one less of his own numbers on the album and because it was below the standard he felt his talents warranted. Goffin and King, of course, were two of rock music's legendary songwriters, albeit not from the 'hippy' era Crosby (and the others) increasingly identified with. The ensuing argument ended with McGuinn literally throwing David Crosby out of the studio, and later informing him that he was out of the band.

They completed the album using session players, who included their original guitarist Gene Clark, plus Michael Clarke, who returned to the fold for one track. When the album was released, the cover picture said it all.

The picture was of what appeared to be a stable with four windows, peering out of the first three of which were Hillman, McGuinn and Clarke. In the fourth was a horse. Crosby simply wasn't there, although he'd appeared on at least half of the album. He was naturally less than pleased, accusing Roger McGuinn of coming up with the horse idea, implying the animal had replaced him in the band.

McGuinn denied it, saying the horse, which belonged to Clarke, just happened to stick its head out when the photo was taken and they liked the result – they'd never actually planned it – and if they had, McGuinn would quip later, 'We would have turned the horse around!'

HENDRIX MEETS THE MONKEES

US, 1967

It seems incredible now but on 8 July 1967, less than a month after their sensational appearance at the Monterey Pop Festival, the Jimi Hendrix Experience embarked on an American tour as support act to the Monkees.

Apparently Hendrix's business manager, Mike Jeffrey, negotiated his involvement in the tour, which was promoted by pop TV producer Dick Clark, because he felt the dates would give the guitarist some national US exposure. Conversely, the Monkees hoped that to be associated with Jimi Hendrix would give them an element of 'hip' credibility.

The Seattle-born guitarist was known to music's inner world as a touring musician and session player, and he had developed a strong following as a performer and a recording artist in England, but stardom in America still eluded him. His fiery performance at Monterey (which he ended by setting his guitar on fire) had brought him a great deal of notoriety, but he still lacked the chart hit (and its attendant radio airplay and media exposure) necessary to make the breakthrough to pop music's top bracket.

The Monkees, though presented in the media via their TV series as a group of whacky American 'mop tops' rumoured to not actually play on their own records, were well aware of the guitarist's reputation. Drummer Mickey Dolenz recalled when he first heard Hendrix in a New York club, 'He was playing lead guitar for the John Hammond band. I'd been invited down to hear "this guy play with his teeth". Sure enough, there was this young black guy who, besides being an extraordinary guitar picker, would occasionally raise the instrument up to his mouth and play it with his teeth.'

Fellow Monkee, guitarist Mike Nesmith, had come across Jimi in even more auspicious circumstances, while having dinner with John Lennon, Paul McCartney and Eric Clapton. 'John was late. When he came in he said, "I'm sorry I'm late but I've got something I want to play you guys." He had a hand-held tape recorder, and he played "Hey Joe". Everybody's mouth just dropped open. He said, "Isn't this wonderful?" So I made a mental note of Jimi Hendrix, because Lennon had introduced me to his playing.'

The next time Dolenz, in the company of Monkees' bass player Peter Tork, came across Hendrix was actually at Monterey and it was there that the idea of a Hendrix–Monkees tour was born: 'It just so happened that we were due to begin our summer tour in a couple of weeks, and we still needed another opening act. When I got back to LA I mentioned Hendrix and his impressive theatrics to our producers. The Monkees was very theatrical in my eyes, and so was the Jimi Hendrix Experience. It would make the perfect union. Jimi must have thought so too, because a few weeks later he agreed to be the opening act for our upcoming summer tour.'

As if to coincide with the unlikely announcement, following hot on the heels of Monterey, that the Jimi Hendrix Experience would be the opening act for the Monkees on a US tour, Jimi incongruously appeared on the July 1967 cover of the teen magazine *Rave*. The paper was aimed at the prepubescent white girls who would pack any concert by the Monkees, despite the latter's move towards creating their own more sophisticated and relevant music for the more 'mature' listeners represented by Hendrix's potential audience.

Hendrix joined the Monkees' tour in progress on 8 July 1967 in Jacksonville, Florida. For the Monkees, it was just an opportunity to watch Hendrix up close, as their producer and songwriter Tommy Boyce confirmed: 'It was a personal trip. They wanted to watch Jimi Hendrix every night; they didn't care if he didn't fit.' As Mike Nesmith enthused, 'The Jimi

Hendrix Experience . . . were the apotheosis of sixties psychedelic ribbon shirts and tie-dye, they had pinwheels for eyes and their hair was out to here . . . I thought, "Man, I gotta see this thing live."'

It was only when the dates with Hendrix got under way that everyone began to realise perhaps it hadn't been such a great idea after all. 'Nobody thought, "This is screaming, scaring-the-balls-off-your-daddy music compared with the Monkees,"' Peter Tork would reflect. 'It didn't cross anybody's mind that it wasn't gonna fly. And there's poor Jimi, and the kids go, "We want the Monkees, we want the Monkees . . ."'

'Jimi would amble out onto the stage, fire up the amps, and break into "Purple Haze", and the kids in the audience would instantly drown him out with, "We want Daavy!" God, was it embarrassing,' was how Dolenz remembered it.

Matters came to head a few days later as the Monkees played a trio of dates in New York. After just a handful of gigs, Hendrix had grown sick of the 'We want the Monkees' chant that met his every performance. Finally, he flipped at the less-than-enthusiastic crowd at Forest Hills Stadium and stormed offstage on 16 July after just seven dates on the road.

Jimi Hendrix had had enough. His single 'Purple Haze' was starting to dent the American record charts and it was time for him to head out on his own and play for audiences who *wanted* to see him. He asked to be let out of his contract, and he and the Monkees amicably went their separate ways.

Reporting the swift end to Hendrix's touring with the Monkees, back in England the *New Musical Express* quoted the guitar star: ' . . . some parents who brought their young kids complained that our act was vulgar! We decided it was just the wrong audience. I think they're replacing me with Mickey Mouse.'

A curious aftermath to the whole affair was when music critic Lillian Roxon mischievously put out a press release to explain Hendrix's abrupt departure from the tour, suggesting that the right-wing group the Daughters of the American Revolution had complained that Hendrix's stage act was 'too erotic' and he was 'corrupting the morals of America's youth', putting

117

pressure on the promoters to dismiss him from the tour. The hoax story was duly printed as a straight news item, introducing a fictitious element to the saga that would be cited as fact for years to come.

THE MYTH OF THE MARS BAR GIRL

WEST WITTERING, SUSSEX, 1967

Of all the stories, gossip and urban myths that arose out of rock 'n' roll in the sixties, none was more widespread than that surrounding the police raid on the Rolling Stones in February 1967.

Even though the facts never supported it, and it was strenuously denied by all concerned, the story of singer Marianne Faithfull and the Mars bar goes down as one of the great pieces of rock mythology.

The well-documented facts were straightforward enough. On the evening of 12 February, the West Sussex Police raided Redlands Farm near West Wittering, the home of Stones guitarist Keith Richards. There, Mick Jagger and Keith were having a party with a number of friends, including Beatle George Harrison, his then wife Patti Boyd, art dealer Robert Fraser and a number of others – including one female who was, according to the newspaper reports, dressed in nothing but a fur coat. The police searched the premises for illegal substances, and found and confiscated a small amount of marijuana plus some amphetamine tablets.

Following the raid, Keith and Mick were arrested – Mick was charged with unlawfully possessing amphetamine tablets, Keith with 'allowing premises to be used for smoking Indian hemp', as the legal jargon put it. But, if the rumour that subsequently circulated was to be believed, the devil, as they say, was in the detail.

According to the version of events on the gossip grapevine at the time, when the police entered the Richards home, the 'girl' in question – always assumed to be Faithfull, then Mick Jagger's girlfriend – had pulled the fur coat around herself as she had been completely naked when the officers of the law arrived. Not only that, the story went, but Jagger (and others present, according to some versions of the legend) was eating a Mars bar that had been strategically placed in Ms Faithfull's vagina. The even more salacious description of events claimed that the confectionery was actually soaked in LSD.

All the Stones later denied the story of course, as Marianne Faithfull herself does to this day, and even though Jagger's beautiful vocalist girlfriend was 'the girl', there was never any hard evidence to suggest the Mars bar story was anything other than a well-travelled urban myth. But it was a myth that did much to substantiate the image of the 'decadent' nature of the 'swinging sixties' in the latter half of the decade.

TELSTAR MAN

LONDON, 1967

One of the most tragic stories in the annals of British pop is that concerning Joe Meek. An innovator who pioneered a new sound from the humble confines of a two-room flat above a leather goods shop in London's Holloway Road, he ended his days a broken man, meeting his eventual end in horrific circumstances.

Born in 1929, Robert Meek had been a radar technician during his National Service in the air force. Upon discharge, he went into television as a sound engineer (he was a lowly repair man for a period) and then into the recording business as a 'balance engineer' at IBC, one of only two independent studios in London in the mid-fifties. While there he worked on records for the Philips and Pye labels, before transferring to the other indie, Landsdowne (for whom he would design a completely new studio).

Meek was the sound engineer on a seminal British blues record (long before the sixties rhythm and blues boom), Humphrey Lyttelton's 'Bad Penny Blues', which made the UK Top Twenty in 1956. Among many other hits he was involved with in the mid-fifties were chart entries by Lonnie Donegan (including 'Gamblin' Man' and 'Cumberland Gap', both chart-toppers), Frankie Vaughan's 'Green Door' (a UK Number Two) and Johnny Duncan's country-skiffle smash 'Last Train To San Fernando' (Number Two in 1957). By the end of the decade Joe was one of the most in-demand producers in the country.

121

In 1960 he launched Triumph, which was Britain's first real independent record label in an industry monopolised by the four major companies: Decca, EMI, Philips and Pye. Ahead of its time, the Triumph label only enjoyed one hit, 'Angela Jones' by Michael Cox, which reached the Number Seven spot in the UK Top Ten in June 1960. Despite no further successes on Triumph, Meek was developing a revolutionary sound in the tiny studio he set up in his flat, now leasing the material to other labels. The chart-topping 'Johnny Remember Me' by John Leyton in 1961 was recorded on second-hand equipment in Meek's bathroom, toilet and living room; it heralded a series of atmospheric hits that may sound dated now but at the time were cutting-edge in their innovative use of effects such as electronic distortion, over-the-top echo and feedback.

Meek had been fascinated by creating weird sounds since, as a teenager, he put up speakers in his parents' cherry orchard to scare away the birds. He was even responsible for building the first TV set in his home town of Newent in rural Gloucestershire. By the time he launched his studio he'd also developed an obsession with outer space and the occult, and was always creating 'sci-fi effects' on his recording equipment; he even recorded an entire other-worldly album around the concept of life on the moon.

But Meek's eccentric leanings towards what sounded like the effects department from a flying-saucer B-movie scored spectacularly with the instrumental 'Telstar' by guitar group the Tornados. Released to cash in on the first communications satellite of the same name, it did just that, as it rocketed up the charts in Britain, America and elsewhere. 'Telstar' made the Number One slot on both sides of the Atlantic in the autumn of 1962, and still sounds oddly 'futuristic' for something from an era when most British pop was nondescript pap. It was a one-off for Joe Meek in terms of worldwide success however, and no sooner had he tasted the real big time (though at odds with his reclusive personality) than the British beat and R & B boom more or less wiped everything that had gone before it off the map.

Joe had other problems too: homosexual, when it was still a crime to be gay, he lived the 'double life' of many at the time. As his musical endeavours became more and more unfashionable, he retreated into an increasingly introverted, tormented world, beset by both personal and financial problems and gripped by increasing bouts of depression.

Claiming he'd had a premonition that Buddy Holly would die on 3 February 1959, things came to a head for Meek (who'd also predicted he would himself die violently before he was forty) early in 1967. On the eighth anniversary of his hero's death on 3 February, in a fit of manic depression he shot dead his landlady then set the gun on himself. His office assistant Patrick Pink would recall how the landlady, Mrs Shelton, went upstairs to see Meek; there were loud exchanges over the rent or lease, after which a shot was fired and the woman came tumbling downstairs – 'Her back was just smoking'. Then, before Pink could do anything, Meek had shot himself outside his control room, 'his head like a burned candle'.

Since his death, Joe Meek's contribution to the progress of record production techniques has been more fully recognised, as has his pioneering of the idea of the independent record producer. In their infancy when Meek made his mark, both developments were pivotal to the changes wrought by the rock revolution of the sixties.

THE UNLIKELY SUCCESS STORY OF TINY TIM

US, 1968

One of the weirdest characters to attract a rock audience following during the hippy era of the late sixties was Tiny Tim, an extraordinary figure at six foot one in height with long curly hair, a prominently large nose and a remarkable – some would say utterly annoying – falsetto voice. His speciality was 'corny' songs from the American popular music of the past, mainly from 1890 to the 1930s, which he accompanied himself on with a tiny ukulele. Generally thought of as a novelty act, he was sometimes derisively referred to as 'the master of the disturbing'.

Born Herbert Khaury, Tiny Tim's year of birth was often unclear – he lied about his age on a number of occasions – and various sources give 1933, 1932, 1930, 1926, 1923 or 1922. However, shortly before his death in 1996, he said he was 64 years old, which would put his year of birth at 1932. This was finally confirmed by photographs of his passport and birth certificate, which stated he was born on 12 April 1932.

Born in New York City, he was the son of a Lebanese father and Jewish mother, and his interest in the popular music of days gone by began at a young age, as did his desire to be a singer, and accordingly he learned guitar and ukulele. He made his performing debut, under the alias Larry Love, in the early fifties. According to legend, it was at a lesbian cabaret in Greenwich Village called the Page 3, where he became a regular attraction. Khaury started to play at small clubs, parties and talent shows under a variety of names; his parents tried to discourage him at first, but relented when they saw that not every gig (though many did) ended in ridicule.

By the early sixties he had acquired a cult following around the thriving Greenwich Village music scene, particularly after he began to incorporate bizarre renditions of contemporary songs into his repertoire. He finally settled on the name Tiny Tim after the character in Charles Dickens' *A Christmas Carol*, which according to some accounts was suggested by a manager previously accustomed to working with midgets!

In 1968 he appeared in the zany rock-documentary movie *You Are What You Eat*, singing an outlandish version of Sonny and Cher's 'I Got You Babe', after which he appeared on the hugely popular TV comedy series *Rowan and Martin's Laugh-In*. He was an instant sensation – whether or not he was seen as an object of ridicule, no one had ever seen anything like him before. He appeared several more times on *Laugh-In*, became a frequent guest on Johnny Carson's *Tonight Show*, and also appeared on the Ed Sullivan and Jackie Gleason TV variety shows.

He was now much talked about, for his eccentric personality almost as much as for his music – he was obsessed with bodily cleanliness and made public his distaste for sex. A record deal was inevitable, and he released his 1968 debut album, *God Bless Tiny Tim*, on the Reprise label. The LP, which sold nearly a quarter of a million copies, included what would become his signature tune, 'Tip-Toe Through The Tulips', that made the US Top Ten when released as a single.

The following year, he recorded and released two more albums, *Tiny Tim's Second Album*, and *For All My Little Friends*, the latter a collection of children's songs. Also in 1969 he married seventeen-year-old Victoria May Budinger (known as 'Miss Vicki' in typically respectful Tim fashion) on the Johnny Carson show, a publicity stunt that attracted forty million viewers. The couple later had a daughter, Tulip, but mostly lived apart, divorcing after eight years.

In August 1970 Tiny Tim made probably the most spectacular appearance of his career, when he performed at the

Isle of Wight Festival in front of a crowd of 600,000 people. His performance, which included English folk songs and rock 'n' roll classics (he'd made the UK Top Fifty the previous year with a version of 'Great Balls Of Fire'), was a huge hit with the predominantly young and trendy audience. At the climax of his set, he sang the old patriotic song 'There'll Always Be An England' through a megaphone, which brought the huge crowd to its feet.

However, in his native US, Tiny Tim's novelty was beginning to wear off and, despite some lucrative gigs in Las Vegas, things were on the slide. Many of his business associates took advantage of his naïveté, leaving him with few savings to show from his run of success, and things got so bad that in 1985 he resorted to joining a circus for eight months. He briefly lived in Australia and then moved back to the States before marrying for the third time, to 'Miss Sue' in 1995 – his second marriage to 23-year-old 'Miss Jan' having lasted for ten years.

Things were looking better by this time, the mid-nineties seeing Tim with two new albums released and regular TV and radio appearances, plus a spot in the Howard Stern movie *Private Parts*. In September 1996, however, he suffered a heart attack while performing at a ukulele festival in Massachusetts. Upon his release from hospital, Tim resumed his concert schedule but on 30 November suffered another heart attack in Minneapolis while performing 'Tip-Toe Through The Tulips', dying an hour later.

The inherent weirdness of Tiny Tim's stage act made him hard to truly appreciate. While audiences were amused by the kitsch quirkiness of his image and delivery, it often never went beyond that, although his genuine love of the material he chose was beyond question. It took the 'openness' of the late-sixties rock scene to accommodate his eccentricity, and give Tiny Tim a far wider public platform than he would have enjoyed otherwise.

AIRPLANE AT ALTAMONT

SAN FRANCISCO, 1969

The Rolling Stones' appearance at the Altamont festival in 1969 is well documented – it's notorious for the fact that Hell's Angels who were supposed to be acting as security during the gig beat a fan to death in front of the stage during the group's set. However, little is read about Jefferson Airplane's similar experience at the same concert.

During the Airplane set at the Altamont Speedway, just outside San Francisco, the Angels (who had been hired in exchange for $500-worth of beer) starting beating up a fan in front of the stage, in a carbon copy of what happened in front of the Stones. But vocalist Marty Balin decided to try to cool things down by jumping into the crowd to intervene, where-upon the pool-cue-wielding bikers turned on him – before jumping on the stage to attack guitarist Paul Kantner as well.

During the chaos, vocalist Grace Slick just carried on singing, 'Ya gotta keep bodies off each other unless you wanna make love,' after which things started to quieten down. When later complimented for the cool way in which she handled the situation, she confessed it was more a question of blindness than bravery, revealing that she had forgotten to put in her contact lenses that morning!

WHO KILLED BRIAN?

HARTFIELD, EAST SUSSEX, 1969

Always considered one of the unsolved riddles of rock 'n' roll, the death of Rolling Stones guitarist Brian Jones continues to attract controversy.

First there are the facts. Twenty-seven-year-old Jones was by 1969 getting more and more distanced from the group he had founded. He was further into serious drug dependence than the rest of the band and as a consequence Keith Richards had become the main instrumental foil to Mick Jagger's vocalising. Jones was becoming unreliable – in the studio, on gigs, musically and socially. Even his celebrated girlfriend Anita Pallenberg had had enough by 1969, transferring her affections to Keith.

Then there were the drug busts. He'd been arrested twice for possession already, and was convinced the police were targeting him for a third time. It was paranoia, fuelled by an increasing intake of LSD and cannabis that also convinced Jones that his fellow Stones were conspiring against him. In this he wasn't mistaken of course, and it was becoming increasingly inevitable that he would be told he was out of the band.

The crunch for Brian eventually came not long after he'd bought a fifteenth-century farmhouse called Cotchford Farm near Hatfield in East Sussex, which once belonged to the writer A A Milne and was the real House on Pooh Corner. Late in June 1969, Brian was visited by Mick, Keith and Charlie Watts, who told him he was out of the band.

Although he had already moved into his new home, Brian was still having it renovated. There was a team of builders employed by a building contractor, Frank Thorogood, carrying out the work – though some reports suggest they got as involved in the ex-Stone's partying as they did in the job in hand.

The other firmly established fact is that Brian, by all accounts staggering and clearly under his usual influence of various drugs and drink, ended up dead in the swimming pool on the night of 2 July 1969. The official verdict was 'death by misadventure', that he had either fallen into the pool or got in difficulties while in the water due to his intoxication. But at least two subsequent reports pointed to the involvement of others in the guitarist's death.

One came via Tom Keylock, a long-time road manager of the Stones who had introduced him to Frank Thorogood. It was claimed in 1993 that Keylock visited his friend Thorogood when the latter was on his deathbed. The builder allegedly told Keylock he had something to get straight before he died, and went on to describe how he 'did Brian' after (not for the first time) losing his temper with the rock star.

There was also another 'confession' on the part of one of the builders, who recalled how there was a lot of drinking going on that night. Brian had his current girlfriend there, a Swedish student named Ana Wohlin, and a female nurse friend of Frank Thorogood's was also present. Brian went into the pool, clearly the worse for wear, and two of the workmen (who had apparently been on his back for weeks) started to tease him, pushing him down under the water: 'it was turning ugly as hell' according to the account. It seems there was one push too many and Brian Jones never surfaced again. Somebody yelled that Brian had drowned, and the builders in and around the pool ran for it.

At the time of Jones's death, the official version – that just Brian, Thorogood and the two girls were there, and they discovered his body at the bottom of the pool after he'd been fooling around in the water – was accepted by most people. That included the rest of the Rolling Stones, none of whom were with the ex-guitarist that night. Why would they be, having just sacked him? And despite Mick Jagger's very public eulogy at the band's Hyde Park concert just three days later on 5 July, only Bill Wyman and Charlie Watts from Brian's old band turned up for his funeral.

CHARLES MANSON, STRUGGLING SONGWRITER

LOS ANGELES, 1969

There was a rumour that went round in the early seventies, not long after Charles Manson was committed to prison for the notorious Sharon Tate murders in 1969, that the mass-killer had unsuccessfully auditioned for the Monkees back in the mid-sixties. But it simply wasn't true – when the pop group was being 'created' for the planned TV series, hundreds did audition before Davy Jones, Mike Nesmith, Mickey Dolenz and Peter Tork finally got the job, but Manson wasn't among them. He was actually in prison, for parole violations arising from previous convictions for car theft and cheque fraud.

Manson did, however, have serious musical ambitions and when he was released from prison in 1967 he made a demo tape with Terry Melcher, the producer of the Byrds' early albums. Manson also approached Neil Young with a view to the singer-songwriter recording one of his songs, and although he never committed a Manson melody to record, Young helped him out to the extent of recommending him to his label Warner's and even giving him a motorbike!

The killer-to-be then took up with the Beach Boys drummer Dennis Wilson, who later adapted a Manson song 'Cease To Exist' for his self-credited 'Never Learn Not To Love', which appeared on the Beach Boys' 1969 album *20/20*. When the album appeared, Wilson would receive death threats from Manson's 'family' of followers.

After the multiple murders of Sharon Tate (who at the time was eight-months pregnant to her husband Roman Polanski) and five others on a two-night killing spree, Manson was convicted for masterminding the slaughter although he didn't actually commit the murders – his 'disciples' in the Manson 'family' (who also got life sentences) did it on his instructions. There were references to the Beatles' 'Helter Skelter' in messages scrawled in blood at the murder scenes, and he always insisted that the song had 'inspired' the killings.

But the 1969 massacre didn't put an end to Manson's musical activity. Via a fellow inmate at the state penitentiary in Concoran, California, where he is still incarcerated, a tape of Charles Manson's songs was released on the Awareness label. And years later, the heavy-metal band Guns 'n' Roses included one of his songs 'Look At Your Game, Girl' on their 1993 album *The Spaghetti Incident*. His songwriting talent may not add up to much, but if Charles Manson had stuck to it as a career option, the world would have certainly been a happier place.

THE INFAMOUS 'TROGGS TAPES'

LONDON, LATE 1960s

One of the most famous bootleg recordings in rock history was not of some unreleased songs by the Beatles or studio try-outs by Bob Dylan, but an infamous compilation of studio chat said to have inspired a sequence in the 1984 spoof rockumentary film *Spinal Tap*.

Known as the 'Troggs Tapes', the recordings were made during a session by British band the Troggs and display, according to *The Penguin Encyclopaedia of Popular Music*, 'instrumental incompetence, mutual recrimination and much foul language'. They would directly inspire the scene in *Spinal Tap* in which Tufnel and St Hubbins have their row in the Rainbow Trout Recording Studio.

Hailing from Andover in Hampshire, the Troggs made a mark on the British music scene with a series of classic singles. Originally called the Troglodytes, the band was started in 1964 by singer and guitarist Dave Wright, bassist Reg Ball, drummer Ronnie Bullis (Bond) and guitarist Howard Mansfield. However, both Mansfield and Wright soon left and were replaced by Pete Staples and Chris Britton from another local band Ten Foot Five. Reg Ball moved from bass to vocals and, on the advice of journalist Keith Altham, changed his surname to Presley. The Troggs line-up was complete.

Larry Page became the band's manager at the beginning of 1966. A first single, 'Lost Girl', was released on the CBS label but failed to chart, after which Page secured a new two-single deal with Fontana. The first Fontana release was 'Wild Thing', which – apart from the infamous tapes, of course – would be the band's greatest legacy. Written by Chip Taylor, originally for a group called the Wild Ones, the song was very different to anything else in the charts with its simple chords, suggestive lyrics and solo played on the ocarina. It was an instant hit in the summer of 1966, reaching Number Two in the UK charts and making the top spot in the United States. The song was subsequently famously covered by Jimi Hendrix.

The follow-up to 'Wild Thing' was 'With A Girl Like You', which topped the British charts, not doing so well in the States as it was released as the B-side of 'Wild Thing'! The group's success encouraged Larry Page to set up his own record label Page One, the first release on which was 'I Can't Control Myself'. On the single, the Troggs featured more of the 'risqué' lyrics that had become almost their trademark, and despite being boycotted if not banned outright by many radio shows it reached Number Two in the UK charts.

The Troggs made two albums during 1966, *From Nowhere* and *Trogglodynamite,* both making the album Top Ten, and had a Top Ten single again with 'Any Way You Want Me' at the end of the year. They had a stab at psychedelia with a 1967 single 'Night Of The Long Grass' that only got to Number Seventeen, then appeared in the Top Five again in October that year with 'Love Is All Around' – the latter being covered highly successfully in 1994 by Wet Wet Wet. And that was about it as far as the charts were concerned, and the band eventually split in 1969, Presley and Bond reforming with two new members in 1972 and doing the rounds of the college and cabaret circuit.

It was during the early seventies that the 'Troggs Tapes' first surfaced, recorded by a bored engineer during a late-sixties session at Page One when the band were having a fierce argument, unaware that the tape machine was running. During the legendary exchanges, the full, unexpurgated tapes revealed over a hundred uses of the 'f-word' in a matter of twelve minutes. In their book, *Rock's Wild Things: the Troggs Files* (published 2000), Alan Clayson and Jacqueline Ryan counted a total of 137 swear words during the animated studio disagreements.

Here's just a sample, as Reg Presley berates the others: 'So, this is what is been going f****** wrong. You've gotta have a f****** bloke that says, "I've got a f****** sound in here that's f****** great! Come in here and have a f****** listen to it." And you come in here and it's probably a different f****** tune, nearly. But if it's f****** good? Yeah, that's it. But when we go through that door, we think, oh f***, no. You know?'

The tapes' notoriety elevated the Troggs to cult status during the punk era, and Reg Presley has been described as 'arguably the first of punk's non-vocalists'. And the tapes did, of course, provide fodder for that memorable scene in *Spinal Tap*.

THE TRUE GODFATHER OF PUNK

NEW YORK CITY, 1969

More so than Lou Reed, who is usually accorded the honour, it is Iggy Pop who was the true 'godfather of punk'. Born James Osterburg in Ypsilanti, Michigan in 1947, he was brought up in the Carpenter Trailer Park, across the road from a shopping centre in the town of Ann Arbour, forty miles from Detroit. After leaving high school and avoiding the draft by pretending to be gay, he formed the Iguanas, from whence came his stage name of Iggy. Short-lived, the group was followed by the Psychedelic Stooges in 1967, soon to be just called the Stooges. Playing the Detroit circuit, they enjoyed a fantastically meteoric ascendance, taking hard rock to masochistic extremes years before punk, and within seven months of their debut performance went to New York to record their first album.

Iggy's stage act was totally outrageous, involving vomiting, stamping on front-row fans' hands and self-mutilation with broken beer bottles that predated Sid Vicious by ten years – this was the peace 'n' love Flower Power era of the sixties! Iggy and the Stooges' debut album, 1969's *The Stooges*, was way ahead of its time; tracks like '1969' (covered by the Sisters of Mercy) and 'No Fun'(covered by the Sex Pistols) voiced an urban angst that was eventually to characterise punk, upon which he was a massive influence. Indeed, the seminal *Punk* magazine that spectacularly chronicled the movement in the late seventies from a New York perspective, featured a cover cartoon of Iggy on its fourth edition in July 1976, the caricature screaming into a microphone, 'I am the world's forgotten Boy!'

136

The Stooges disbanded in 1970 after their second album *Fun House* and, despite his most celebrated champion David Bowie persuading them to reform for *Raw Power* in 1973, Iggy's lifestyle was too extreme for the mainstream rock world represented by the English glam-rock idol. Later collaborations with Bowie (including *The Idiot* in 1976 and *Lust For Life* in 1977) produced arguably his best – though in many ways least risky – work. His most famous output was often via others, notably 'Nightclubbing', covered by Grace Jones and 'China Girl', co-written with and later recorded by Bowie. But his most profound impact was on what would become punk in its earliest real manifestation in groups like the New York Dolls, and later bands that would follow them on both sides of the Atlantic.

THERE'S A RIOT GOIN' ON

RICHMOND, VIRGINIA, 1969

There have been rock 'n' roll riots, and rock 'n' roll riots, but one at a gig featuring the Steve Miller Band must have been among the most spectacular. The occasion was the Cherry Blossom Festival in Richmond, Virginia in 1969, the venue a local football stadium.

There were about ten bands on the bill, and the promoters had had assurances from the local police and the mayor that everything would be OK, so everything looked good.

When Miller and his group arrived there were about 25,000 people on the football field itself, with no one actually sitting in the stadium. The first two bands' sets went down without any problem but, while the third act was on stage, trouble erupted in the audience.

According to Miller, there were two hundred plain-clothes narcotics agents in the audience who had started busting people. Then, while Boz Scaggs (who had recently left the Miller band) was playing his set, a helicopter soared overhead, thirty feet above the audience, tilting sideways so the judge inside could see for himself the people in the crowd smoking pot. Next, buses arrived, out of which poured armed police, which Miller described as 'storm troopers with four-foot shields, big poles and helmets, everything'.

Next door to the football park a new stadium was under construction, and a kid from the crowd managed to scale a dirt ramp on the building site and start up a bulldozer, which he then drove down the ramp at breakneck speed, crushing at least seven police cars. It was then that fans started smashing the windows of the police vehicles.

Meanwhile, it was time for Miller's headlining set, and the promoter was urging him, 'You've gotta play, man. You've gotta go up and play!' even though mayhem had broken out. The riot police had now entered the stadium, preparing to charge into the crowd, who responded by hurling cans and bottles at them.

It was then that Miller pulled off a show-stopper. He dedicated the next number to the police, and proceeded to play a version of 'The Star-Spangled Banner', whereupon the law officers took their helmets off and just stood there in respectful silence. The riot was suddenly no more, and the Steve Miller Band finished their set, and the concert.

PAUL IS DEAD

DETROIT, 1969

One of the most celebrated urban myths in rock 'n' roll was the 'Paul is dead' Beatles rumour that spread like wildfire in October 1969. The story was initially broadcast by a Detroit DJ, Russ Gibb, who said a listener had phoned him and made the claim.

According to the legend, Paul McCartney had been killed in a car accident back in late 1966, just as the band were recording what would be their new single and the *Sgt Pepper* album. Manager Brian Epstein and the other three Beatles had supposedly covered up the incident, replacing Paul with a lookalike – a Scotsman called William Campbell – who underwent plastic surgery to complete the transformation. The surgeons involved, however, failed to fix a scar on Campbell's upper lip – this is supposed to be how you can tell 'authentic' McCartney photos from the 'Campbell' ones.

For reasons best known to themselves, the band decided to drop various 'clues' in their subsequent records, the most famous being on the next single, 'Strawberry Fields Forever', released in February 1967. If the record was played backwards, so the claim went, at the end you could hear John saying 'I buried Paul' (in fact he was saying 'cranberry sauce') – and the Detroit DJ did just that to substantiate the story.

From then on, the rumour mill went into top gear, and fans all over the world were playing songs backwards and scouring record covers to uncover more 'clues'. Among the most widely circulated of these was that Paul was walking barefoot on the cover of *Abbey Road* (which had only been released a week or so before the notorious broadcast), suggesting the other three were a funeral procession. On the same picture, the car in the background has a number plate '28 IF', the age Paul would have been *if* he had lived! And Paul is smoking with his right hand, though the real McCartney was left-handed, indicating that an impostor was brought in for the photograph.

In 'A Day In The Life' the line 'he blew his mind out in a car' had obvious connotations, even though it was widely known to refer to a friend of the Beatles, the Guinness heir Tara Browne, who *did* die in a motor accident while possibly (though it was never proven) 'tripping' on LSD. And the very appearance of the so-called 'White Album' – white representing death in some quarters – was seemingly another giveaway. Likewise on the *Sgt Pepper* cover, Paul's uniform has a patch that appears to read 'OPD' (Officially Pronounced Dead), but in reality it says OPP, standing for 'Ontario Provincial Police'.

At least two books have been published about the legend, and a number of websites still perpetuate the controversy today. And another myth, which was a by-product of the original rumour, was that the Beatles had started the whole story themselves, as it was certainly – in John Lennon's own words at the time – 'a great plug for *Abbey Road*!'

THE LED ZEPPELIN SHARK TALE

SEATTLE, 1969

The most famous rock 'n' roll legend of all involving on-the-road sexual excess is without doubt the infamous 'mud shark' legend, which relates how members of Led Zeppelin supposedly employed a live shark as a sexual device with a compliant female groupie. There are a number of different versions of the story, but it's probably safe to say that it springs from a true incident that has been variously embellished over the years.

Variations on the tale involve some or all of the members of Led Zeppelin, and the fish in question has been variously quoted as a shark, a mud shark, a swordfish or a red snapper. The creature is said to have been alive, dead or stuffed and mounted, while the groupie is sometimes said to have been tied (at her own instigation) to the bed.

The incident on which the legend was based took place in July 1969 at The Edgewater in Seattle, a smart hotel on Puget Sound from which guests could fish right out of the windows of their rooms. According to Led Zeppelin's road manager Richard Cole, he and drummer John Bonham were busily engaged in catching sharks through a bedroom window, when they were interrupted by some persistent groupies, but what occurred next wasn't quite as extreme as the legend would have it.

Cole's version of events claims that the fish employed wasn't even a shark, but a red snapper. The groupie in question happened to be a redhead, and Cole set about pleasuring her with the head of the fish while Bonham watched. According to Cole, the girl was completely happy with the entire episode and left the hotel unharmed in any way.

Given that Cole's accounts of the wild goings-on with the band were prone to exaggeration, it's reasonable to assume that his version of the 'shark' myth is as near to the truth as it gets. Whatever – over the years, the Led Zeppelin 'shark tale' in all its variations has persisted as one of the enduring pieces of rock mythology.

LET IT BAKE

LONDON, 1969

When artist Robert Brownjohn was commissioned in 1969 to design the cover for a new Rolling Stones album, he came up with the idea of having a specially cooked and designed iced cake sitting on top of a tyre, a can of film and a clock face. This would all apparently be balancing on the spindle of an old-fashioned automatic record player that was 'playing' a Stones album. The album was at that stage to be called *Automatic Changer.*

Brownjohn did some rough sketches for the idea and showed them to Keith Richard, who liked the idea, so Brownjohn arranged to shoot it the following week on a budget of £1,000. Looking for someone to actually cook the cake, he contacted a freelance food economist – the lady in question was working for a food photographer and had just started a column in the *Daily Mirror.*

'It was just another job at the time,' the cook recalled later. 'They wanted it to be very over-the-top and as gaudy as I could make it.' Recording engineer George Chkiantz, who had been working on the album, remembered the circumstances: 'She was shacking up with a bloke who was staying at a friend of mine's apartment.' According to Chkiantz neither the food journalist nor her partner had that much idea what to do – 'It was this friend of mine who told them how to cook a sponge cake.'

If the cake-baking lady was that inexperienced, she certainly got her act together subsequently. The album, of course, was eventually called *Let It Bleed*, while the then-obscure creator of the sponge marvel was none other than TV chef and best-selling food writer Delia Smith.

THE LEGENDARY MASKED MARAUDERS

SAN FRANCISCO, 1969

One of the great hoaxes of rock 'n' roll – which in fact developed into a double spoof – featured in the early days of *Rolling Stone* magazine, in October 1969. Earlier that year, what is reputed to be the first true bootleg album had appeared, a collection of unreleased Bob Dylan material entitled *The Great White Wonder*, and the magazine had run an article about the album's sales. Following that, rock writer Greil Marcus, under the pseudonym of 'T M Christian', wrote a fictitious review of an album called *The Masked Marauders*.

The review claimed that the Masked Marauders were in fact a 'supergroup' consisting of Mick Jagger, Paul McCartney, John Lennon and Bob Dylan, who'd got together to record an album that couldn't be released under their real names because of contractual ties to a variety of different record companies. This explained why, supposedly, fans had not heard of the album (allegedly produced by Al Kooper, another star name) prior to its release, as the whole project had to be recorded in secret.

There were plenty of indications that the review was just a put-on, with humorous items including Mick Jagger singing 'I Can't Get No Nookie' and Bob Dylan singing a number ('Season Of The Witch') by the notoriously Dylan-influenced Donovan. But despite this, and 'facts' such as the session was supposedly recorded 'in a small town near the site of the original Hudson Bay Colony in Canada', a lot of readers simply missed the joke and actually went asking for the album at their local record stores.

As demand for the non-existent record escalated, Marcus took the joke a step further with his fellow *Rolling Stone* critic/editor Langdon Winner by putting together a group of Berkeley musicians to record a collection of songs matching those described in the review – right down to imitating the voices of the famous singers alleged to be involved. After receiving some local radio airplay, the tape was eventually bought by Warner Bros. Music, and released as an album on their Reprise label. To give the album full 'authenticity', it was released under a Reprise/Deity banner, 'Deity' being the fictitious label named in the original hoax review.

Even though the record carried just a picture of a woman on the front and no pictures of the 'Masked Marauders' or identifying information about them on its outer sleeve, there were plenty of fans seemingly taken in by the hoax. There was even an inner sheet included with the album which made it clear that the whole thing was a send-up, but eager fans still insisted they could recognise Dylan's voice, McCartney's bass playing and the rest, just anywhere. They must have felt doubly stupid when eventually *Rolling Stone* itself exposed the whole thing as an inspired practical joke.

There was a déjà vu element to the story in 1988, when George Harrison formed a Marauders-like band called the Traveling Wilburys with Bob Dylan, Tom Petty, Roy Orbison, and Jeff Lynne, all of whom were identified with pseudonyms using the surname 'Wilbury' on the album sleeve.

GRACE SLICK AT THE WHITE HOUSE

WASHINGTON, 1970

Jefferson Airplane (and later Jefferson Starship) vocalist Grace Slick was one of the most prominent figures in the US 'alternative' society of the late sixties and early seventies – her first band, presumably with a touch of irony, was called the Great Society. As part of that very anti-establishment movement, she espoused a highly liberal attitude to sex, drugs, the war in Vietnam and life in general. She was a proto-feminist too, and counted amongst her friends prominent political activists, some of whom were recognised as thorns in the side of the establishment.

It seemed incredible, therefore, when a rumour began to circulate that in April 1970 Slick had not only been invited to the White House wedding party of President Richard Nixon's daughter Tricia, but while she was there managed to spike the drinking water with LSD, causing everyone to hallucinate. The rumour, alas, was untrue, but did have its basis in fact.

Born Grace Wing in 1939, when she was a still a nice middle-class girl from the Chicago suburb of Evanston, Illinois, Slick had attended the Finch College in New York from 1956 to 1958. Richard Nixon's daughter Tricia was also a student at straight-laced Finch (which Slick would describe as a 'bow and curtsey academy'), though some years later than the rock star, and in 1970 was chosen to host a tea party with former graduates of the college at the White House.

Even though a security screening took place, an invitation to the April event was sent to Grace Slick, who immediately saw it as an opportunity to make some mischief of one kind or another. Her first step in that direction was to let the organisers know that her 'escort' for the party would be 'Mr Leonard Haufman', better known as the left-wing activist and 'yippie' (post-hippie radicals) propagandist Abbie Hoffman.

The two hatched a plan whereby they would drop some pure 'acid' (LSD) into the President's coffee cup, but from Slick's subsequent account of the escapade in her book *Somebody to Love?* it seems the pair couldn't have seriously expected to get in to the smart-set soirée. Hoffman dressed for the event in a suit and tie, with slicked-back hair, 'looking like a hit man for the Mafia', while Grace had on a fishnet top, short black miniskirt and long black boots. She recalled that they looked like, 'a pimp and a go-go girl'.

When they got to the White House, Grace and Hoffman were both immediately recognised by the security men, who told Slick she was on an FBI list as a security risk. The security folk eventually gave in, telling Slick that as an invitee she could enter, but not her escort. The two conspirators both made their exit at that point, the LSD still on their persons as they hadn't actually been searched. Apparently both the President's wife Nancy and his daughter Tricia wanted to meet Grace when they heard she was there, but by that time Slick and Hoffman had beat a hasty retreat. And needless to say, contrary to rumour Grace Slick wasn't invited to Tricia Nixon's wedding bash, which took place a few months later.

BOB DYLAN, STREET FIGHTING MAN

NEW YORK CITY, 1970

A J Weberman was a notorious Bob Dylan follower who made the singer's life a misery by hanging round his house in New York's Greenwich village in the early seventies, bringing hordes of like-minded 'fans' to hang outside the address at 94 MacDougal Street, and famously picking through Bob's garbage for snippets of information.

Weberman became known for his new 'science' called garbology, in which he went through the subject's rubbish in order to gather scraps of evidence to support his theories – whacky theories about Dylan's work, and how the folk-rock legend had been the subject of CIA brainwashing so that he ceased to write anti-war and other 'political' songs anymore.

Dylan was as patient as possible with the zealous Weberman, repeatedly asking him to leave him and his family alone, granting him phone interviews, and even offering him a job as his chauffeur – which Weberman refused for unknown reasons. But in 1970, things came to a head some months after the Dylans had moved into their house, when A J led forty or so hippie followers that he lectured in a 'Dylanology' class to Bob's home, where they screamed for Dylan to 'crawl out yer window', and answer charges that he had been co-opted, chanting slogans like 'Dylan's brain belongs to the People, not the Pigs!'

The 'protesters' blocked the street, and Dylan could take no more. A few days later, Weberman was there again, going through the garbage, when Dylan's wife came out, shouting at him to clear off. According to Weberman, 'Dylan said if I ever f***** with his wife, he'd beat the shit out of me.' Two days later, Bob did just that, finally losing his temper. 'He's little, but he's strong,' Weberman would recall later. 'He works out. I wouldn't fight back, you know, because I knew I was wrong. He gets up, rips off my "Free Bob Dylan" button and walks away. Never says a word.'

HOW DID JIMI DIE?

LONDON, 1970

After just three years at the top, guitar supremo Jimi Hendrix was found dead in a London hotel room on 18 September 1970, and from that day on the circumstances surrounding his death have been the subject of rumour, conjecture and controversy.

Hendrix first made the big time in the UK, rather than his native America, early in 1967 when he made the Top Ten with 'Hey Joe'. He followed through with other hits and broke in his homeland a few months later, with a sensational debut at the Monterey International Pop Festival in June '67, the now-legendary event that heralded the 'Summer of Love'.

By the end of the year Jimi was an international superstar, though in a classic case of too much, too soon, a high-powered schedule of touring and recording was already beginning to take its toll. On 4 January 1968, during a gruelling European tour, Jimi cracked for the first time, when a combination of fatigue, acid and booze resulted in him smashing up a Gothenburg hotel room. He was arrested for criminal damage.

But the treks continued at the same pace, and although rifts began to show in his band, The Jimi Hendrix Experience, the three-piece managed to stay together – not least because they were the highest paid group on the circuit. Not that they saw much of the money. When their original manager, ex-Animals bass player, Chas Chandler, relinquished half their management to a wheeler-dealer called Mike Jeffrey, the band began to ask where their huge fees were actually ending up. When they weren't too stoned to care, of course.

And the pressure continued into 1969 when a dispute with a former manager led to all of Hendrix's American royalties being frozen. This didn't stop him disbanding the Experience, however, and forming a new five-piece, A Band of Gypsies, with whom he planned to record a double album at his newly built Electric Ladyland studios in New York in August 1970.

Manager Jeffrey, however, had other ideas, and interrupted the recording sessions with a hastily arranged European tour which included an appearance at the 1970 Isle of Wight Festival. After the 1969 event with Bob Dylan, the Isle of Wight bash was being heralded as the 'British Woodstock', and it certainly had a lot in common with its American counterpart in terms of chaos. Dogged by problems over money, security and whether fans should enjoy a 'free festival', the shows seemed doomed by 'bad vibes' before they started. Jimi's set was no exception, and he was momentarily relieved to move on to another less contentious festival a few days later in Germany.

But the German date was even more traumatic for the Hendrix band, as bass player Billy Cox nearly had a nervous breakdown after someone spiked his drink with LSD. The rest of the Continental dates were cancelled and Hendrix returned to London, where although he had a suite at the smart Cumberland Hotel, he stayed at the Notting Hill flat of Monika Danneman, a Danish skating instructor he'd met while he was on tour in Germany.

On 15 September, Hendrix and Danneman were in Ronnie Scott's club in Soho when a fracas erupted involving another of Jimi's girlfriends, Devon Wilson, during which Wilson allegedly kicked the Danish newcomer out of her chair. Two nights later, Hendrix attended a party thrown by the Who's manager Kit Lambert in the company of Devon Wilson.

Between 1.30 and 2 a.m., Monika Danneman – who later claimed that Hendrix had asked her to marry him – collected the guitarist from the party. According to her version of what happened next, the two of them stayed up talking for hours until she fell asleep in Jimi's arms. Waking up at around 10 a.m., she went out to a local shop to buy cigarettes, returning to find Hendrix still asleep but with 'something dripping out of the corner of his mouth'. When she couldn't wake him up, she rang singer Eric Burdon (a friend of Jimi's) to try and get the name of Hendrix's doctor, then dialled 999 for an ambulance. Before the medics arrived, she tidied up what she described as 'incriminating evidence' and noticed that eight or nine of her sleeping pills were missing. She went on to claim that the ambulance crew didn't seem at all worried about Jimi's condition when they saw him.

However, in her book *Rock Bottom*, Pamela des Barres quotes an interview with journalist Tony Brown in which the ambulance men recall something quite different. Claiming only Hendrix was there when they arrived at the flat, one described the scene as horrific, with Jimi covered in vomit – they said they knew he was dead as soon as they saw him.

Danneman would also claim she rode in the ambulance to the hospital, another fact disputed by the crew and later also discounted in the official enquiry. And Monika would insist that hospital staff told her that Jimi might recover, then after being told he was dead was allowed to see the body. Hospital records, however, stated Hendrix was 'dead on arrival' and staff would recall that his body was identified by his roadie, Gerry Sickells.

There are uncomfortable anomalies as to the time when Jimi was found to be ill. The roadie would insist that Monika rang him some time before 9 a.m., and Burdon recalled that he heard from her 'at the crack of dawn'. The ambulance records, however, point to it not being called until after 11 a.m. A question mark has remained ever since as to what happened in the time between.

Danneman went on to tell her story in a book, *The Inner World of Jimi Hendrix*, in 1995, after which another ex-Hendrix girlfriend, Kathy Etchingham, sued her for libel. The court found Monika Danneman 'in contempt', and two days later she was found dead in her Mercedes car, asphyxiated by carbon monoxide. And the trail of fatalities didn't end there. Less than two years later, Devon Wilson died in suspicious circumstances after falling from a window in the Chelsea Hotel in New York City.

WHEN KRIS CRASHED IN ON CASH

NASHVILLE, 1970

Singer Kris Kristofferson swept into the music business in more ways than one, on a career path that was nothing if not convoluted.

A Golden Gloves boxer early on, he attended Pomona College in California from whence he gained a Rhodes scholarship to study literature at Oxford. Joining the air force, he went on to be made a captain and acquired a pilot's licence. After moving to a teaching job at the West Point military academy, Kristofferson suddenly resigned in 1965 when he decided to take up songwriting seriously, earning a living meanwhile as a commercial helicopter pilot.

Next stop was Nashville, where he swept the floors of a recording studio just so he could make contact with some industry names, which he did when one day he buttonholed none other than country giant Johnny Cash. The superstar somewhat reluctantly agreed to listen to some demo tapes that the ambitious floor sweeper gave him, but Kristofferson later heard that Cash was actually dumping them in a local lake.

Undeterred, Kristofferson came up with his most audacious plan yet. During a training flight, he swooped in on Cash's home and landed the 'chopper' in the yard, handing over a second batch of tapes in person. Cash would later recall how Kristofferson almost fell out of the helicopter because he was so drunk, with 'a beer in one hand and a cigarette in the other'.

It was just as well that this time the plan paid off. Another inebriated flight saw the singer-songwriter lose his piloting job after passing out at the controls, but meanwhile Cash recorded Kristofferson's 'Sunday Morning Coming Down' – which may well have been a reference to the 'copter landing. Whatever, the song went on to be voted the 1970 'Song of the Year' by the Country Music Association and Kris Kristofferson was finally on his way up.

SYD BARRETT, ROCK RECLUSE

CAMBRIDGE, 1970–2005

Syd Barrett was the phenomenally talented founder of Pink Floyd, but after just two years at the centre of the sixties 'psychedelic' rock scene, has lived as a recluse ever since. Having last given an interview in 1971, Roger Barrett, as he was born in 1946, has avoided any contact with the media or fans since then. Although he was at the cutting edge of the so-called 'swinging London' music scene, back in 1966.

By October of that year, Barrett was already well on the way to stardom. His band Pink Floyd had supported Soft Machine at a launch party for the magazine *International Times*, a two-thousand-strong star-studded gathering that involved lots of LSD, Marianne Faithfull dressed as a nun and Paul McCartney disguised as an Arab.

The group got some encouraging press reviews, and began to take off. The first of the capital's 'flower children' began to throng to hear Syd's forty minute freak-outs, the lights and general weirdness establishing Pink Floyd as Britain's first 'psychedelic' band.

The promoter Joe Boyd, who had some production experience, took them into a recording studio in late January 1967. Barrett had written 'Arnold Layne' by then, and perfected the relentless riff of 'Interstellar Overdrive'. EMI signed them up on the basis of these demos, choosing 'Arnold Layne' as the first single. Barrett was delighted. 'We want to be pop stars,' he said, gladly grinning for cheesy publicity shots. However, by April, Syd was complaining about the record company demanding more commercial material. 'Arnold Layne' had only been out six weeks, and already Syd was beginning to resent the light-hearted ditty. He hated playing note-perfect, three-minute renditions on stage every night but that didn't stop it charting at the end of April.

On 29 April, the band headlined at Britain's biggest psychedelic happening ever, the '14-Hour Technicolor Dream' at the cavernous Alexandra Palace. It was a drug-driven affair. Floyd's co-manager Peter Jenner was tripping on acid that night, and Barrett probably was, too. There were forty bands, dancers and strobe light shows entertaining a 10,000-strong audience.

But already the growing excesses of a hallucinogenic lifestyle were beginning to take their toll on Syd Barrett. Cambridge pal and future Floyd member David Gilmour would recall, 'Syd didn't need encouraging. If drugs were going, he'd take them by the shovelful,' although the Floyd's bassist Roger Waters once said that, 'Syd was being fed acid.' The guitarist/vocalist also smoked copious quantities of marijuana, and had a penchant for Mandrax tranquillisers.

A July tour of Britain didn't help things, when fans just shouted for their two hits 'Arnold' and 'See Emily Play' ('Emily' had made Number Six in June). Barrett hated the pressure, as did the rest of the band, but reaction was far more negative. He would detune his Fender until its strings were hanging loose, and hit one note all night; or stand staring straight ahead while the others performed as a three-piece. Perhaps Barrett was making a statement, or pushing experimental 'free music' to new limits, but what was clear was that he was becoming seriously mentally ill. All the band realised it, almost certainly including Syd himself.

Things were looking increasingly fragile on stage, concerts becoming shambolic. Although their debut LP *Piper at the Gates of Dawn* was released on 4 August, their agents Blackhill Enterprises cancelled the next three weeks' gigs and arranged a Mediterranean holiday for them all. The *Melody Maker* ran a front-page story headlined PINK FLOYD FLAKE OUT.

A US mini-tour in November 1967 was a disaster. With huge venues, and louder-than-loud bands, Barrett's whimsical tunes seemed totally out of place, not that he seemed to care that much. When they arrived in Los Angeles, he'd forgotten his guitar – 'It's great to be in Las Vegas,' he said to a record company man.

After the American debacle, the band began thinking of how to replace or augment Syd, who was now hardly communicating. They set off on a British package tour with Hendrix, the Move, Amen Corner, the Nice and others, playing two 17-minute sets a night for three weeks, with three days off in the middle. Predictably, the schedule was too much for Barrett, who sometimes failed to show up at all, Dave O'List of the Nice standing in for him.

By the end of the year the other three members of Floyd hatched a plan: they would ask David Gilmour to cover lead guitar and vocals while Syd could do what he wanted, so long as he stood onstage. Barrett couldn't care less, and Gilmour leaped at the chance, having a week of rehearsals with the band before they went back on the road. Driving out of London for a gig, someone said, 'Shall we pick up Syd?' to which the others replied, 'F*** it, let's not bother.' Syd Barrett would never work again with the band that he founded.

Undoubtedly, Syd felt hurt by the way he'd been treated. He would turn up at Floyd gigs ready to go on stage, only to be rebuffed, even standing at the front, staring out Gilmour as his old friend played his guitar licks. Pete Jenner tried to get Barrett involved in new 'solo' projects through 1968, to no avail, and by the autumn he'd become homeless, living at his mother's in Cambridge.

Syd's downward spiral continued, alleviated briefly in 1970 when he made two solo albums, the well-received *When the Madcap Laughs* and *Barrett*. A few chaotic gigs followed, after which he laid low in an increasingly troubled mental state.

In the early eighties Barrett spent time in a psychiatric hospital, then a charitable institution, Greenwoods, in Essex. During that time he distanced himself from his previous life as a rock star. On the death of his mother Win in 1991, Syd destroyed all his old diaries and art books. Since then, he's regularly warded off innumerable fans, journalists and others seeking him out, and remains the ultimate rock recluse, the Howard Hughes of the psychedelic generation.

JIM MORRISON R.I.P.

PARIS, 1971

When the legendary Doors vocalist Jim Morrison died in Paris on 3 July 1971, his actual demise was shrouded in mystery. He'd grown tired of fame and sought anonymity in Paris with his long-time girlfriend Pamela Courson. His health was already in decline and he was excessively overweight. Morrison was found dead in the bath, probably from a heart attack induced by a drug overdose, but few people saw the corpse except for Courson and an anonymous doctor, thus fuelling a rock legend that he'd faked his own death.

He was buried (we're assuming the legend was just that) in the famous Père Lachaise Cemetery, which houses the remains of the great and famous, from Bizet and Chopin to Oscar Wilde and Edith Piaf. But after the rock star was interred there, the grave, which remained unmarked for many years, became a place of pilgrimage for thousands of fans, much to the concern of the local authorities that look after the rambling cemetery.

A stone block was placed over his sealed grave after many attempts to unearth the body were made by followers of the occult, who came from around the world, allegedly performing devil-worship rites, and staging sexual orgies and drug parties at the grave site. Fans even came over the walls at night, and security guards with dogs patrolled the grounds while cameras to survey the grave were installed, along with night lighting. Litter, wine bottles, drug needles and graffiti were left behind, as well as the usual tributes of flowers, poems and such. Souvenir hunters took everything that could be uprooted or

162

torn free, including a stone head of Morrison that had been erected on the grave at some point. The French were so concerned about the disturbance that Morrison's continued presence created there, that in 2001 they tried to have the body moved back to America, when the thirty-year lease on the plot had run out.

Fast forward now to 2003, in the Los Angeles apartment of rock journalist Brett Meisner. Looking through some old photographs, he comes across one taken some years earlier by the singer Tom Petty – it's Meisner posing in front of the Morrison grave at Père Lachaise. Looking closer, there in the background, he could see a shadowy figure that certainly wasn't present when the picture was taken, and which he'd never noticed before when he'd looked at the photo. Meisner could only speculate that this was some supernatural apparition – the ghost of Jim Morrison no less! He subsequently had the picture tested by an FBI photo lab, who declared it one hundred per cent genuine – there was no evidence of it having been tampered with.

Then Meisner thought on – there in his flat he actually had the stolen 'head' from Morrison's grave, which he'd come by via a collector some time before. The mystery that still haunts him is whether Jim's 'ghost' on the photograph appeared before or after he'd acquired the tombstone relic.

LENNON BUSKING IN NEW YORK CITY

NEW YORK CITY, 1971

'I should have been born in New York, I should have been born in the Village. That's where I belong. Everybody heads towards the centre and that's why I'm here now. I'm here just to breathe it.' So said John Lennon after moving to his adopted 'home town' of New York City, where he would meet one of the seminal influences of his post-Beatles life, the poet, singer and political activist David Peel.

With his childhood memories of Liverpool coloured by nostalgia (having lived in London since the Beatles' first chart success in 1963), for ex-Beatle John Lennon the similarities between the overtly working class, unpretentious yet culturally dynamic port of his birth and the city of New York perhaps appeared sharper than to others. On the other hand, having grown up in the war-scarred and austere Britain of the forties and fifties, New York also represented a glamour once only hinted at through Hollywood movies and rock 'n' roll.

Whatever his reasons, when he took up residence there in 1971, not long after the break-up of the biggest band in the history of rock 'n' roll of which he was a part, Lennon felt he was 'coming home', so great was his affinity with the metropolis. For Lennon, New York simply *was* the ultimate rock 'n' roll city.

In August 1971, John and his wife of two years, Yoko Ono, left their palatial home in the English countryside, Tittenhurst Park, and took up residence at the St Regis Hotel, on the corner

164

of 55th Street and Fifth Avenue. But right from the start Lennon was drawn to Greenwich Village, and soon became familiar with the open-air poetry and music sessions that had been a feature of Washington Square since the late fifties. It was here he was to meet David Peel.

Once considered the 'Woodie Guthrie of Yippie Politics', Peel was an anarchistic poet/singer who believed that all music should be free of charge, and performed around the parks and streets of Manhattan to prove his point. He'd already released an album in the mid-sixties called *Have A Marijuana*, recorded live on the streets of New York with his loose band the Lower East Side, and when he spotted the Lennons in the crowd as he sang 'The Pope Smokes Dope' in Washington Square, it was the beginning of a relationship that led to Lennon producing an album of the same name for the Beatles' Apple label. The release of the album propelled Peel into celebrity (followed by cult) status, given the extremely rare (dis)honour of being banned by virtually every country in the world, except America and Canada.

Tracks like 'I'm A Runaway' and 'I'm Gonna Start Another Riot' were a precursor to the pre-punk street-fightin' stance adopted by Lennon during his sojourn in the Big Apple, and the former Beatle even brought Peel on stage during a 1972 concert at Madison Square Garden, as well as once joining in 'busking' as part of Peel's street band. In a subsequent album, with the Apple Band and released on his own Orange label, Peel included an interview in which Lennon described how they met, and what attracted him in the New Yorker's music:

'Howard Smith was showing Yoko and me around the Village – although Yoko didn't need any showing – but he was an old friend of Yoko's and I got to know him. And he took us down to Washington Square of course, and *there he was*, you know, shouting about "Why do you have to pay to see stars?" and all that, and I'm standing at the back of the crowd feelin' all embarrassed, thinkin', "He must be talkin' about me – he must know I'm here!" But he didn't. And then we walked off.'

'Another time . . .' Lennon continued, telling how he played for free in the streets of New York, 'it was arranged for us to meet him, but it seemed like a happening . . . he was just suddenly there, and we started singing with him in the street. We got moved on by the police and it was all very wonderful and that was it . . . We loved his music and his spirit and everything, and his whole philosophy of "the street", so we thought, "well, OK, let's make a record with him." '

And Lennon actually namechecked Peel on the first album he completed after moving to New York, *Some Time in New York City*, singing on the title track: 'His name was David Peel, and we found that he was real.'

The Lennons moved to their first apartment in New York after three months at the St Regis. Yoko Ono had already lived in Greenwich Village (she had been a resident of the city since the fifties, establishing herself a reputation as part of New York's avant-garde) and John took an instant liking to the neighbourhood, so they moved into 105 Bank Street in the West Village, just vacated by the Lovin' Spoonful drummer Joe Butler and next door to composer John Cage.

David Peel described to writer Steve Turner, in the UK *Independent* newspaper in 1990, how John Lennon's eighteen months as a Village resident were a period of relaxed freedom, when he could walk the streets, cycle around, go to local shops and enjoy a freedom he hadn't experienced since the early sixties – with or without any busking: 'It was after the break-up of the Beatles and before the government really came down on him, it was the calm before the storm. Yoko used to cook excellent macrobiotic food and they used to have some great suppers at Bank Street. I have to say I think it was one of the happiest times of their lives.'

JAGGER SLEEPS WITH BOWIE

LONDON, c. 1972

It was on US television's *Joan Rivers Show* on 4 May 1990 that Angela Bowie decided to spill the dirt on her famous ex-husband – a ten-year gagging order that had been imposed as part of their divorce agreement having just expired.

Rivers had tantalisingly promised her audience that her guest was 'ready to dish – and I mean down and dirty dishing – about her ex'. But it seems Angela suddenly got cold feet and decided that she didn't like 'kissing and telling' after all, whereupon she was led off camera and scornfully denounced for her cowardice by the talk-show host.

Thinking things over, the ex-Mrs Bowie returned to the set and discussed her stormy marriage with rock's 'Thin White Duke' claiming, 'I caught him in bed with men several times. In fact, the best time I caught him in bed was with Mick Jagger,' this being when she walked into her bedroom after returning from a trip. When asked by her fellow guest, radio personality Howard Stein, if the two men had their clothes off, she answered, 'They certainly did.'

Although she didn't elaborate on when the incident occurred, or offer any further details – other than to comment that her immediate reaction to the discovery was to go and make breakfast – the implications of her revelation were crystal clear. David Bowie had long since openly acknowledged his bisexuality and although Mick Jagger had not made any such admission (along with his known dalliances with scores of women), rumour had it

167

that the Rolling Stone wasn't necessarily a hundred per cent heterosexual.

And the fact they were both naked pointed to one thing. If they'd crashed into bed after a night out on the town that was one thing, even stripping down to their underclothes would be understandable. But two men of variable sexual persuasion in bed together without a stitch on looked far more suspicious.

As would be expected, Mick Jagger was quick to dismiss the whole thing as 'complete rubbish', and a public letter from David Bowie's lawyer stated that any 'implication that there was ever a gay affair between Mick Jagger and David Bowie is an absolute fabrication'. And within a week Angela Bowie was tempering her story, claiming that although what she had revealed was literally true, it didn't necessarily mean what people assumed it meant.

Then, on the *Geraldo Rivera Show* daytime chat programme of 11 May, she spelled things out: 'I certainly didn't catch anyone in the act. All I found were two people sleeping in my bed. They happened to be naked and they happened to be Mick Jagger and David Bowie and it's not a big deal. It doesn't mean necessarily that it's some sort of affair.' A few months later she was already dismissing the gossip as 'old news', claiming that the two rock superstars were only 'passed out in bed'.

That would have seemed to be the end of the matter, even though the rumours wouldn't go away, until Angela Bowie shook things up once again in her 1993 book *Backstage Passes*. In the tell-all autobiography, she poured scorn on the public for assuming what she had obviously intended to imply, while at the same time admitting that she actually *still* believed what everyone else had assumed! And nobody, save for Mick and David, will ever really know.

DOUBLE DEATH IN MACON

MACON, GEORGIA, 1972

Tragedy hit sixties Southern rock band the Allman Brothers on 29 October 1971, when guitarist and founder member Duane Allman was killed in a motorcycle accident. While in Macon, Georgia, during a band break from touring and recording, Duane was riding toward an oncoming truck; it was turning well in front of him but then stopped mid-intersection. He lost control of his Harley-Davidson Sportster motorcycle while trying to swing left, possibly striking the back of the truck or its crane ball. Flying from his bike, it landed on top of him and skidded with him, crushing internal organs; Duane died a few hours later.

After Duane's funeral and a few weeks of mourning, the five surviving members of the Allman Brothers Band carried on with the name, going back on the road and making more highly successful albums.

Just over a year later, on 11 November 1972, an eerie second tragedy hit the Allman Brothers Band when their bass player Berry Oakley was involved in a similar smash. He was riding his motorcycle with one of the band's road crew when they collided with a bus – and it was also in Macon, Georgia, just three blocks from where Allman met his fate.

Friends took Oakley to the same hospital Allman was treated at, but he died from head injuries and internal bleeding later that night. The 24-year-old Oakley was buried next to Allman with a matching tombstone, in the Civil War section of Macon's Rose Hill Cemetery.

CARLY'S VANITY MAN

US, 1972

One of the best-kept secrets in the music world concerns Carly Simon, her song 'You're So Vain' and whom exactly it's about. From the moment it first appeared on her 1972 album *No Secrets* there was speculation as to the identity of the man in the song, with its cutting chorus line 'You're so vain, I'll bet you think this song is about you,' and when it was released as a single and a worldwide smash it became more of a popular guessing game among music fans. Was it her ex-boyfriend Warren Beatty, or her husband at the time, James Taylor? 'No, it's definitely not about James, although James suspected that it might be about him because he's very vain,' Carly would tell *Rolling Stone* magazine in 1973. How about Mick Jagger then, he appeared singing backing vocals on the record, maybe his vanity got the better of him and he agreed to be on the session because he knew there was a song about him? 'No,' Simon has insisted over the years. Ex-boyfriend Cat Stevens, ex-boyfriend Kris Kristofferson? The answer's always been negative, but after over thirty years Carly knows she can let this one run and run.

In 2003 she even appeared in a charity auction, creating an intense media buzz when she offered to reveal the identity of the person(s) she had in mind when she penned the song to the highest bidder, but only after they agreed to abide by a confidentiality agreement. Shortly after this news was printed in *People* magazine, the *Associated Press* picked up the story, and newspapers, television and radio shows around the world immediately followed.

The news lines on all the major cable networks began carrying Carly's 'name' across the bottom of the television screen. MSNBC.com conducted a viewer's poll where Beatty's name secured 54 per cent of the vote. Matt Lauer reviewed the list of usual suspects with Anthony DeCurtis (of *Rolling Stone*) on *The Today Show*. Roger Friedman of *Fox News* went on record with his firm opinion that the song was about Warren Beatty. The BBC's *Up All Night* radio show interviewed Carly fans live from the US to get their opinion on whom the song was written about, and why this mystery has such long-lasting appeal.

On 4 August, the auction price hit $50,000 for Carly's 'Dream Secret'. The winner and nine of his friends got to join Carly at her home, for a reception at which she sang 'You're So Vain' (naturally) while her guests enjoyed peanut butter and jelly sandwiches and vodka on the rocks. Then, at midnight, the winner alone got to learn Carly's closely guarded secret. Later he gave one clue out to the rest of the world – 'The letter "E" is in the person's name.'

DEBBIE HARRY'S NARROW ESCAPE

NEW YORK CITY, *c.* 1973

In the early seventies, around the time she was about to make her mark on the Manhattan scene with her first New York band the Stilettoes, future Blondie vocalist Debbie Harry had a terrifying experience that could well have seen her on the list of victims of a notorious serial killer.

It was late at night on the Lower East Side, and Debbie was trying to get a cab to an after-hours club she frequented. A small white car drew up and the male driver offered her a ride, but she ignored him and just continued to try to flag a cab down. However, the guy was very persistent and he asked where she was going. When she replied that it was only a couple of blocks away, he said, 'Well I'll give you a ride.'

Debbie half-reluctantly got into the car and, as she was soon to realise, this was a big mistake. It was summertime, yet all the windows were rolled up, leaving about an inch and a half at the top so, as the car started off, she automatically reached down the side of the door for the winder, only to realise there was no door handle, no window winder, nothing at all. Apart from the seats, the inside of the car had been totally stripped out.

Now she was starting to panic. 'I got very nervous,' she would recall in a 1989 newspaper interview. 'I reached my arm out through the little crack and stretched down and opened the car from the outside. As soon as he saw that, he tried to turn the corner really fast, and I spun out of the car and landed in the middle of the street.'

The driver, Harry was convinced more than fifteen years

later, was almost certainly serial killer Ted Bundy, who was executed in January 1989 in the electric chair in Florida. Through the seventies he had sexually assaulted then killed many young women across the country, and eventually confessed to thirty murders, though estimates run to over a hundred.

It was right after his execution that Debbie read about Bundy and, although she hadn't thought about her nasty experience in years, it all made scary sense. The whole description of how he operated and what he looked like, the kind of car he drove and the time frame he was doing it in all fitted exactly. She said to herself, 'My God, it was him.' In retrospect she felt it was 'Very scary . . . truthfully, I hadn't thought of the incident in fifteen years. I'm one of the lucky ones.'

'KEEF' CLEANS UP

SWITZERLAND, 1973

Rolling Stone Keith Richards has been the subject of more myths over the years than most rock stars. Most persistent, especially during his years of heavy substance abuse (that is, right through the seventies), was that Keith was rumoured to be dying. And even today, many assume that because his body was abused for so long and is therefore prematurely 'old', he surely must be in poor health. These days nothing is further from the truth apparently, with the old rocker on a no-drink-or-drugs health and fitness regime.

The other great 'Keef' myth involves the drug detox he undertook in 1973. The legendary guitar man was so deep in the throes of a heroin addiction that he reportedly took drastic measures to clean up prior to an important European tour. There is little to deny that Richards underwent treatment in Switzerland, but what is disputed is the nature of the treatment. While it was most likely a haemodialysis process that filters impurities from the bloodstream, fans have often maintained that the guitarist had a complete blood transfusion, like a premature embalming. It didn't help that Richards once told a journalist that, yes, he had in fact undergone a complete transfusion. 'I was just fooling around,' he would admit years later, 'I was f***ing sick of answering that question so I gave them a story.' The rumours were further fuelled in 1978 by an unaired skit on the American TV show *Saturday Night Live* in which Keith stated that, 'Every February I have to go to Switzerland to get my blood changed.'

ABBA AGAIN

SWEDEN, 1974–81

Between winning the Eurovision Song Contest with 'Waterloo' in 1974, and their break-up in the early eighties, Abba were one of the biggest success stories in pop history. At the height of their fame they were Sweden's biggest export, exceeding even Volvo cars, and a 1977 concert at London's Royal Albert Hall attracted 3.5 million applications for just over eleven thousand available tickets.

With US record sales of 20 million, and UK sales of over 25 million, estimates of the quartet's total worldwide sales vary from anything between 140 and 500 million. And it's safe to say that a huge proportion of these figures reflect sales since the group's disbandment over twenty years ago. The fact that in 2000 Abba apparently turned down an offer of a billion dollars to do a reunion tour attests to their continuing popularity, as does the phenomenon of spin-offs that have far outlasted the original group.

To date, Abba have only permitted two artists to actually sample their music: the Fugees, who sampled 'The Name Of The Game' for their 1996 track 'The Rumble In The Jungle', and Madonna, who did the same with 'Gimme Gimme Gimme (A Man After Midnight)' for her 2005 single 'Hung Up'. But the plethora of covers by other artists over the years has guaranteed the Swedes huge royalties, even if they never sold another record from their own back catalogue.

Synth-pop duo Erasure had considerable success in 1992 with an EP of Abba covers, *Abba-esque*; the music video for their version of 'Take A Chance On Me' featured the group members dressed in drag as the female half of Abba, Agnetha and Anna-Frid. In the same year, a UK studio tribute-group that specialised in techno and house remakes of many original Abba hits was put together under the name Abbacadabra.

But it's the live tribute bands that have been the real Abba phenomenon of the nineties and noughties, ranging from Sweden's A Teens to the cleverly named Super Troopers. There's Abba Alive from Germany, the Agnetha and Anna-Frid tribute duo Abbagirls, Canada's AbbaArrival, Abbasolutely Live from the UK and (another great pun) Abbalanche from Australia.

And it's Australia that has given the world the most famous Abba tribute band of them all – Björn Again. Formed in 1989, they had become so successful by 2004 that there were five casts of Björn Again performing in various parts of the world. At the time of writing the original Björn Again have been touring for sixteen years, twice as long as the original group existed.

BRUCE SPRINGSTEEN – THE FUTURE OF ROCK 'N' ROLL?

BOSTON, 1974

Just as a respected critic had stuck his neck out and put his reputation on the line back in 1961, when *New York Times* critic Robert Shelton had raved about the young Bob Dylan, giving a definite kick-start to his career, so it was in 1974, when Jon Landau declared, 'I saw rock 'n' roll's future, and its name is Bruce Springsteen,' first in the Boston *Real Paper* (he'd gone to a concert in Boston where Springsteen already had a cult following) then in the May edition of *Rolling Stone* magazine:

> When his two-hour set ended I could only think, can anyone really be this good: can anyone say this much to me, can rock 'n' roll still speak with this kind of power and glory? . . . Springsteen does it all. He's a rock 'n' roll punk, a Latin street poet, a ballet dancer, an actor, a poet joker, a bar band leader, hot-shit rhythm guitar player, extraordinary singer and a truly great rock 'n' roll composer. He leads a band like he's been doing it forever . . . Bruce Springsteen is a wonder to look at: skinny, dressed like a reject from Sha Na Na, he parades in front of his all-star rhythm band like a cross between Chuck Berry, early Bob Dylan and Marlon Brando. Every gesture, every syllable adds something to his ultimate goal – to liberate our spirit while he liberates his by baring his soul through his music.

Heady stuff, yet Landau's 'rock 'n' roll's future' must have become one of the most quoted lines in rock music history, but in many ways it was true, albeit not in the way that the critic necessarily intended.

What talent-spotting critics and A & R men everywhere were looking for in the early seventies was the next name to raise rock back to its status at the cutting edge of youth (though not necessarily teenage) culture, as it had been when the Beatles and/or Bob Dylan were the driving force. Springsteen was being inaccurately touted as the 'new Dylan' when Landau heard about the buzz he'd been creating through the previous year, but his 'rock 'n' roll' description was more true in the literal sense – Springsteen was harking back to an older, basic rock tradition that had its roots in white R & B bands of the sixties like the Young Rascals, the early manifestations of British R & B, and the fifties rock 'n' roll that had inspired both.

The only son of a working-class family in the decaying seaside resort of Asbury Park, he played rhythm guitar with a variety of local bar bands including the Castiles and Steel Mill, the latter seeing him firm up a working relationship with guitar player 'Miami' Steve Van Zandt at the beginning of the seventies.

Springsteen formed the E Street Band in 1972, which Van Zandt would later join, but meanwhile also played the Greenwich Village circuit as a solo singer-songwriter; the latter was the context in which he was spotted by Columbia's John Hammond. The result was *Greetings from Asbury Park NJ* (with a cover featuring picture postcards of the seen-better-days town) in 1973. The album included acoustic tracks alongside those accompanied by the band, whose loose sound with the honking sax of Clarence Clemons harked back to the R & B-tinged rock of outfits like Gary US Bonds.

However, the album didn't make the breakthrough it was hoped for, not helped by the fact that the hype was talking about a 'new Dylan' which the record – even the acoustic tracks – simply didn't reflect. But what it did reflect was what people saw at Springsteen's gigs, leading to a burgeoning reputation as a live act which saw a local following emerge across the southern States and other localities including Boston, where Landau experienced his Damascus-style conversion.

Produced by Springsteen's manager Mike Appel *Asbury Park* included the nucleus of the regular backing band in saxophonist Clarence Clemons, bass player Gary Tallent, David Sancious on keyboards and Vini Lopez on drums. Although it featured the hits-to-be 'Blinded By The Light' and 'Spirit In The Night' (which both charted for Britain's Manfred Mann), the true sound of Springsteen and the band at that time was more accurately captured in the follow-up later in 1973, *The Wild, the Innocent and the E Street Shuffle*. With the stage favourites 'Rosalita', 'New York Street Serenade' and the riveting 'Sandy (Asbury Park, Fourth of July)' this is the album that sums up the Springsteen experience as witnessed by Landau.

Reviewers of the album, most of whom hadn't come across the debut collection, raved about a voice they compared variously to Van Morrison and Wilson Pickett but if anything, the LP was constrained by over-long lyrics (as in the epic 'Incident on 57th Street') which further confused the issue of whether Springsteen's songwriting aspiration was indeed to be the 'new Dylan'.

All was rectified, however, with *Born to Run* in 1975, which was his first album to chart on release and contained in the title track his first hit single. As his two previous LPs now appeared in the best-seller lists and his picture appeared in the same week on the covers of *Time* and *Newsweek* (which headlined 'Rock's New Messiah'), Bruce's time, it seemed, had come. 'Born To Run', 'Thunder Road' and 'Night' were hailed as instant classics, and with 'Miami' Steve Van Zandt now on guitar, he toured Europe for the first time.

Touring became the main thrust of activity, as a management dispute and subsequent court injunction with Appel prevented him entering a recording studio for the next three years. During that time the concerts became the stuff of legend – three- to four-hour marathons featuring not only his own material but tributes to the very spirit of rock 'n' roll with covers of hits by the likes of Buddy Holly, Chuck Berry, Gary US Bonds and even Britain's Searchers.

This didn't keep his name out of the charts, however; other artists who had hits with his songs included Patti Smith with 'Because The Night', the Pointer Sisters with 'Fire' (actually written for Elvis Presley, who died before recording it) and Southside Johnny and the Asbury Jukes with 'The Fever'. Then, in 1978, Springsteen was back in the studio – now under the management and production auspices of long-time supporter Jon Landau – where he made *Darkness on the Edge of Town*, altogether starker and more brooding than his previous offerings, but a milestone all the same.

Landau may have revised his view about his now-client being 'the future of rock 'n' roll', but his prediction certainly fitted the essence of Springsteen's music better than the impossible-to-live-up-to aspiration of being called 'the new Bob Dylan'.

THE BOGUS FLEETWOOD MAC

LONDON, 1974

Fleetwood Mac were famous for the inner-band politics and personal relationships that accompanied their 'golden period' that began when they relocated to California in 1974. That was when Mick Fleetwood, John McVie and Christine McVie were joined by guitarist Lindsay Buckingham and vocalist Stevie Nicks, which heralded two chart-topping albums – and a series of affairs within the band that were as celebrated as their music.

But the personnel changes in the outfit, which had started as a UK blues band back in 1967, were just as convoluted in their earlier days.

First their founder-member guitarist Peter Green suddenly left the band in 1970, after an LSD-induced 'bad trip'. Green was replaced by pianist and vocalist Christine Perfect who, by the time she had become a fully fledged member in 1971, had married bass player John McVie. That same year, as they toured America, their other founder-guitarist Jeremy Spencer disappeared – the band later discovering that he left to join the religious cult, the Children of God.

Next to go was guitar player Danny Kirwen, who was fired in 1972 after breaking down on stage, to be replaced by guitarists Bob Weston and Dave Walker. Walker left in 1973, and Weston was fired after having an affair with either John McVie's wife Christine or Jenny Fleetwood (Mick's wife) – reports vary. In the ensuing chaos music and personnel-wise, the band scrubbed the rest of a US tour and returned to London.

Their manager Clifford Davies was, as would be expected, furious – so much so that in 1974 he actually put together a bogus Fleetwood Mac to fulfil the cancelled dates in the United States. A number of London-based musicians were sent anonymous telegrams inviting them to phone a certain number; the call then told them about a top-secret audition that was taking place. The musicians who passed the audition were told they could join Fleetwood Mac. In this way, Davies put together a line-up consisting of no real members of Fleetwood Mac – to tour the States as Fleetwood Mac!

The American Mac fans weren't best pleased, demanding to see the real group that they'd paid for – threats were even made against some of the 'bogus' band; and, in London, Mick and John were appalled to hear on the grapevine that Fleetwood Mac were currently touring the USA.

The real Fleetwood Mac filed and won a lawsuit against the impostors, who, after losing in court, began performing under the name Stretch – but the legal wranglings kept the real band off the road for most of the year. In the meantime Mick, John, Christine and co moved to California, where a 'new' – but genuine – Fleetwood Mac would emerge, with phenomenal results.

GOODBYE MAMA CASS

LONDON, 1974

Keen to make even the most tragic of situations more sensational, a combination of tabloid media, rock 'n' roll press and over-prurient fans has been known to turn many a star's sad demise into nothing more than ghoulish gossip.

A case in point was the death on 29 July 1974 of 'Mama Cass' Elliott of the Mamas and the Papas at the age of just thirty. Cass actually died of a massive heart attack, undoubtedly brought on by her weight problem and possibly the crash diets she undertook to combat it. Yet when her body was discovered in a London apartment during a solo concert tour – the group had split up in the late sixties – all manner of theories as to how she met her end began flying around.

One, inevitably, was that she died of a heroin overdose. Another, rather luridly recalling Jimi Hendrix's passing, said she had asphyxiated on her own vomit. The most imaginative, if one wanted to look at it that way, was the proposition that she had died while miscarrying John Lennon's baby. But the version of her death in most common currency at the time was that she choked while eating a large ham sandwich in bed – and it's even found its way into some of the rock 'history' books over the years.

One bit of rock 'n' roll trivia that doesn't get into most of the history books is the fact that the apartment where she died – Flat 12, 9 Curzon Place – was owned by the singer Harry Nilsson, and was the same top-floor flat where the Who's drummer Keith Moon died in 1978.

183

THE LOUD AND SHORT OF IT

NEW YORK CITY, 1974

When New York punk band the Ramones first hit the city's rock 'n' roll scene in 1974, they immediately impressed everyone for two reasons – the volume at which they played, and the speed of their delivery.

When they debuted at CBGB's, the catalyst venue for American punk, the club's proprietor Hilly Kristal was startled at the salvo of numbers, all less than two minutes long – they played twenty songs in seventeen minutes without a stop.

In fact, during those early days in their career, Joey Ramone and his band-mates often had altercations with nightclub managers because they played so fast. After a gig in Rhode Island one evening, a club owner called the local sheriff to complain that he (and the audience) hadn't had their money's worth. The Ramones retorted that they had in fact played the requisite set, while admitting that they had cut out their usual banter between numbers. The owner felt he had good reason to complain, given that the quartet had played their 22-song set in just twenty minutes.

And in addition to the crackling guitar sound and machine-gun delivery, they were loud – for their time, *very* loud. Kristal still remembers how one of the top female stars of the seventies, Linda Ronstadt and her entourage, came 'slumming' to hear the Ramones and see what all the fuss was about. 'I got them right up front, but they lasted less than five minutes. She literally flew out of the door holding her ears.'

The Ramones played so loud that when they were recording their first album, 1976's *Ramones*, they destroyed several pieces of studio equipment that just couldn't take it. But their greatest rock 'n' roll moment came during a concert in 1977, in Marseilles, France: Joey and the boys played full volume – and allegedly used so much power that they blacked out the entire city!

THE HIGHS AND LOWS OF BADFINGER

UK, 1970s

When the Beatles set up their Apple label in 1968, with the intention of signing new acts as well as releasing their own material, it would have seemed like the chance of a lifetime for any individual or group who were given the backing of the Fab Four. But the association with the superstar group didn't always spell out-and-out success.

Their first hit on the label by another artist was with Mary Hopkin, who shot to the top of the UK chart (and Number Two in the USA) with 'Those Were The Days' in 1968, though subsequent hits failed to have the spark that made her debut so commercially memorable. The label's most prominent album artist, James Taylor, only really hit the mark after he'd moved from the Beatles' label (with whom he released *James Taylor* in 1968 with George Harrison and Paul McCartney guesting) to Warners in 1969.

Even one of Apple's most consistently successful signings, Badfinger, were dogged by bad luck which ultimately led to a bizarre double misfortune. Badfinger were a tight, technically brilliant vocal-instrumental group from South Wales, originally known as the Iveys. They were managed by Bill Collins, whose son Lew Collins had played in the Merseybeat group the Mojos before finding greater fame as actor Lewis Collins in the TV series *The Professionals*. Bill Collins was a time-served Liverpool bandleader, and a friend of Paul McCartney's father Jim.

186

After a single on Apple as the Iveys in 1968, 'Maybe Tomorrow', the group changed their name to Badfinger because they apparently thought the Iveys sounded 'too Merseybeat'. With the new name came some personnel changes, and the line-up settled with founder Pete Ham plus Liverpudlian Joey Molland on guitars, Tom Evans on bass and Iveys original Mike Gibbons on drums. They were taken under the personal wing of Paul McCartney and had three consecutive hits in the US and UK Top Ten with 'Come and Get It' written by McCartney, 'No Matter What' (both in 1970) and the McCartney-penned 'Day After Day', produced by George Harrison, in 1971. And an even longer-lasting mark was made with the Ham and Evans composition 'Without You', a worldwide smash (and Number One on both sides of the Atlantic) for singer Harry Nilsson in 1972.

Badfinger, perhaps not surprisingly, sounded very Beatles-like, and this undoubtedly filled something of a gap for fans after the 1970 disbandment of John, Paul, George and Ringo. There was even a rumour circulating that their records were in fact the reformed Beatles under an assumed name, and the band was only put together to substantiate their disc successes.

But the group made some ill-advised business decisions outside the seemingly charmed orbit of the ex-Beatles, involving Stan Polley, an American manager with alleged affiliations to the Mafia, who saw to it that little of their money ever came their way.

Things got so bad financially that Pete Ham, married with a child and another on the way, was unable to pay the bills or even his mortgage. On 23 April 1975 the guitarist hanged himself in the garage-cum-studio at his home in fashionable Weybridge, leaving a cryptic note in a music book with the PS, 'Stan Polley is a soulless bastard. I will take him with me.'

The band predictably broke up after that, but Tom Evans soldiered on for the next eight years in various reunion tours, including a 1978 line-up with Molland and Yes keyboard player Tony Kaye. All were financially disastrous, and Evans spent more time fighting court cases and legal threats than enjoying any fruits of his earlier fame.

Eventually, he, like Ham before him, could take it no more, and on 18 November 1983, he too was found hanged from a tree in his garden. The initial magic of the Beatles' touch could do nothing to prevent the later curse that seemed to bedevil Badfinger, on a downward spiral from perhaps too-instant fame to a double tragedy.

THE EARLY DAYS OF THE SEX PISTOLS

LONDON, 1975

The formation of the Sex Pistols, which was a catalyst for the whole media explosion surrounding British punk rock, has usually been characterised as their Svengali-like manager, Malcolm McLaren, 'putting the group together' after Johnny Rotten had wandered into his clothes shop on London's Kings Road.

In fact, the band's history goes back some time before that, to a group called the Strand (in reference to a song by Roxy Music), which was formed during 1972 by drummer Paul Cook, vocalist Steve Jones and Wally Nightingale on guitar. During 1973, the band members began to frequent a fifties-style retro clothes shop called 'Let It Rock' in the Kings Road, run by ex-art student Malcolm McLaren and his partner Vivienne Westwood. Jones, aware that McLaren had some connections in the music business, asked if he would be interested in becoming the group's manager, although at the time McLaren declined. And it was in the shop that they met Del Noone, who they recruited to play bass. By 1974, the group were calling themselves the Swankers, and played their very first gig at a birthday party of a friend of Cook's at Tom Salter's Café in London. They also began rehearsing in a studio called the 'Crunchy Frog', near London's docklands. It was shortly after this that Noone left the band, as he became unreliable and didn't turn up for rehearsals.

189

The other three were now looking for another bass player and found him in Glen Matlock, who stayed as a permanent member until replaced by Sid Vicious in 1977. By early 1975, Jones and Nightingale were in serious disagreement about what direction the band should take, the result being that Nightingale left the group, with Jones taking over on guitar.

It was then that John Lydon entered the picture. He was another client at McLaren's shop, which had now been renamed and restyled as the 'SEX' boutique, and he deeply impressed McLaren and the proto-Pistols when he walked into the shop in August 1975 wearing a home-made T-shirt emblazoned with 'I Hate Pink Floyd'. Asking him if he was interested in joining them, the only 'audition' involved him miming to Alice Cooper's 'Eighteen', which he passed.

McLaren became the new group's manager, and was asked to think of a name for the outfit. Among the possibilities voiced were Le Bomb, Subterraneans, the Damned, Beyond, Teenage Novel, and QT Jones and his Sex Pistols. The 'QT Jones' was dropped, and the Sex Pistols were born. Although the name suggests the male sex organ, McLaren later stated that he wanted the band to be 'sexy assassins'. Under their new manager's guidance, the band was initially influenced in part by the simple, chord-based style of the New York Dolls (who he'd briefly managed) and the Ramones. McLaren had given guitarist Jones the Les Paul guitar used by New York Doll Sylvain Sylvain, and the torn-shirt, spiked-hair look of Richard Hell, then the bass player for Television. All these figures were prominent on the New York City punk scene and later new wave scene. Rotten (as it was decided Lydon would be called) and his circle of friends walked into the arrangement already possessed of a similar sartorial style – a grunged-out version of the 'soul boy' fashion affected by fans of Roxy Music. McLaren would also claim at this stage – perhaps with a touch of irony, perhaps not – that he wanted the Sex Pistols to be 'the new Bay City Rollers'.

The band played their first gig under their new name at St Martin's School of Art in London on 6 November 1975, a reportedly chaotic affair that was followed by other dates at colleges and art schools for the remainder of the year. In early 1976 they began playing at London clubs (like the 100 Club in Oxford Street) and pubs such as the Nashville. After their first concert outside of England, on 3 September 1976, when they played at the opening of the Club de Chalet du Lac in Paris, they embarked on their first major tour of England, which lasted from mid-September to early October (including a gig at Chelmsford Prison), which got them noticed by EMI. The rest, as they say – including the group being dropped by the label just three months later – is history.

THE ROD STEWART PARTY MYTH

LONDON, MID-1970s

One of the most outrageous stories ever to circulate on the rock 'n' roll rumour network was started in the mid-seventies, concerning a most unlikely candidate: professional 'ladies man' Rod Stewart. The gritty-voiced singer was said to have been rushed to hospital after swallowing the semen of a large number of fellow party guests. Where or when the party actually took place seemed to alter with each telling of the tale, but the myth persisted enough for Rodney to comment on it in an interview in *Rolling Stone* magazine in 1991. Declaring the rumour never hurt his womanising reputation in the least, he himself wondered who the gang of revellers could have been whom he'd supposedly serviced so prodigiously – a fleet of sailors, or a football team perhaps?

Apparently almost identical stories have abounded since the early part of the twentieth century, when the silent-movie star Clara Bow was similarly rumoured to have been involved with the entire University of Southern California football team, which at the time included future Hollywood legend John Wayne! Other rock and pop stars who have featured in similar tales of indiscretion with varying numbers of people have included Elton John, David Bowie, Mick Jagger, Jon Bon Jovi, the Bay City Rollers and, more recently, Lil' Kim, Britney Spears and Fiona Apple.

THE KILLER AND THE KING

MEMPHIS, 1976

It was like a scene out of a *film noir* movie, as a car pulled up outside the mansion, lights dimmed and then switched off. The occupant of the Lincoln Continental that had just drawn to a halt didn't move – he just sat there, waiting outside the wrought-iron gates. The guards posted at the gateway went to investigate, and found a familiar figure brandishing a bottle of Jack Daniels bourbon in one hand and a .38 pistol in the other. 'You just tell him the Killer's here,' he slurred as he wound down the window. The guards recognised the prowler immediately – it was Jerry Lee Lewis, the self-styled wild man of rock 'n' roll. The mansion, of course, was Graceland, and the Killer had come to visit the King.

It wasn't the first time that Memphis-based Jerry Lee had arrived at the gates late at night, demanding to see his old label-mate and rock 'n' roll rival Elvis Presley. Just the evening before, on 22 November 1976, he'd driven his Rolls-Royce to Graceland, just south of Memphis on Highway 51, a mile or so from the Mississippi state line. It was 2.50 in the morning, and he was told the King was asleep, whereupon he drove off and some time later crashed his Rolls. He was arrested for reckless driving, driving while intoxicated, and driving without a licence.

This time Elvis was awake, and when the security guards rang up to the house telling him what was going on, Presley simply instructed them to call the police. The police arrived, and not for the first time – or indeed the last – Jerry Lee Lewis, as drunk as he was the night before, was led away in handcuffs.

DRAG QUEEN ATTACKS WRESTLER

NEW YORK CITY, 1976

When the New York punk scene developed in the mid-seventies, there was a friendly rivalry between the two main venues involved, CBGB on the Bowery and Max's Kansas City on Park Avenue. There was one incident, however, that threatened to divide the scene between supporters of one club or the other. Now passed into legend, the fracas that ensued at CBGB in March 1976 involved Wayne County, the punk drag act, and 'Handsome' Dick Manitoba, lead singer with one of CBGB's punk regulars the Dictators.

County had been a part of the scene since its inception; along with the New York Dolls he was responsible for introducing a trash-drag element into punk. He had played regularly at a sleazy venue called Club 82, where his outrageous act was extreme even by punk standards. He would perform wearing skintight dresses, a false vagina with fake pubic hair, and even a massive dildo with which he did things on stage that could only be referred to obliquely in print reviews. He'd started doing gigs at CBGB and at Max's, where he was also the house DJ.

Accounts of the incident at CBGB varied widely, as they still do to this day. According to County's version of events, Dick Manitoba – who was apparently also a wrestler – started heckling his act, calling him a 'drag queen', 'queer' and such. The transvestite vocalist replied by inviting his protagonist up onstage to say it to his face. The Dictator did just that, brandishing a beer mug threateningly. County acted quickly, swinging the mike stand and catching Handsome Dick on the collarbone with its heavy base, sending the macho punk reeling into a table on which he cracked open his head. Mayhem ensued on stage as Manitoba leaped at Wayne, the two exchanging punches, the latter's wig and dress spattered with blood. And, as in all good club fights, the band played on. Manitoba was taken to hospital by ambulance, where he had sixteen stitches and was treated for a broken collarbone.

The New York *Village Voice* newspaper immediately saw the humorous side of it all, running the headline: MAD DRAG QUEEN ATTACKS POOR DEFENSELESS WRESTLER, while the local musical community found itself siding with one or other of the injured parties. More or less everyone agreed that County had overreacted – apparently Manitoba never actually hit him, though he looked like he was about to – but there was little sympathy for the homophobic rantings of the Dictators singer. The police subsequently had a warrant out for County who was eventually apprehended when he arrived at his DJ job at Max's wearing a male wig, false moustache and beard! The case, brought by the Dictator's managers, was eventually thrown out of court.

For many bands, it was prudent to side with Wayne over the affair, if only because his manager Peter Crowley booked the acts into Max's. The Dictators were blacklisted by Crowley, who put pressure on other club owners not to book them. But the biggest result of the whole business as far as fans were concerned came on 30 May with the New York Party in aid of County's Legal Defense Fund, featuring a line-up that included Richard Hell, Blondie, Johnny Thunders, Tuff Darts and Cherry Vanilla.

EAT YOUR HEART OUT

DENVER, COLORADO, 1976

On the evening of 1 February 1976, Elvis Presley was at home in the Graceland mansion entertaining two guests: Captain Jerry Kennedy of the Denver police force and Ron Pietrafeso who was in charge of Colorado's Strike Force Against Crime. Elvis had a personal interest in law enforcement; he'd even been made an honorary member of various police forces around the country. On this occasion, however, as they chatted about policing in Colorado, Elvis's mind wandered – he suddenly remembered that Colorado was the home of the best sandwich he'd ever eaten – the legendary Fool's Gold.

Elvis had sampled the sandwich only once, when after a concert he was invited to a restaurant called the Colorado Gold Mine Company in the Denver suburbs of Glendale. He'd ordered the house speciality, named Fool's Gold on account of its outrageous price – $49.95. And the first bite alone was enough to make a lasting impression on Elvis.

Now, a few months later, Elvis was reminded of those sandwiches. He started talking about how sensational they were and, as both his guests were from Colorado, they were doubly intrigued. Elvis had a policy when entertaining: his guests' wishes, however bizarre, were his command. It might be a swim in the pool at four in the morning, or a visit to a Memphis hamburger joint at midnight, but now he found himself keeping Fool's Gold as the topic of conversation, even though it might mean a thousand-mile trip to Denver.

Drooling at the thought of the sandwich, one of the two lawmen eventually said, 'Boy, I wish I had me one of them now!' and that was the only signal the King needed. Almost before they knew what was happening, the Colorado cops were seated inside a stretch Mercedes along with some more of Elvis's buddies, being whisked to the Memphis airport. Elvis's personal jet, the *Lisa Marie*, was waiting for them on the tarmac.

Meanwhile, at the Colorado Gold Mine Company, the scene was one of organised panic. The call had come from Memphis at midnight, and the cooks had less than two hours to meet their deadline. The huge griddle was scrubbed clean in order to fry up the massive quantities of bacon required, as they prepared the 'takeout' of a lifetime. The food was ready just in time, and the restaurateur, his wife, and a waiter rushed to Denver's Stapleton airport with 22 sandwiches plus the rest of the order, which comprised a case of Perrier, a case of champagne and a chest of cracked ice. The *Lisa Marie* landed at 1.40 a.m. and taxied to a private hangar. The food was presented to Elvis on silver trays, and the feasting went on for two hours.

So what exactly is Fool's Gold? The super-size sandwich consists of an entire baguette-style loaf, smeared with butter then browned in the oven. When it's warm the loaf is sliced lengthways and hollowed out, and filled with coatings of peanut butter and strawberry jam (a whole jar of each per loaf) plus a pound of crispy-fried bacon. It's eaten just like that, while the bacon's still hot. The total calorific count for just one is reckoned to be 42,000 calories, and once he got into the habit of them after the Denver outing Elvis would regularly have two for his evening dinner. Eat on!

DISCO FEVER

NEW YORK CITY, 1977

Brooklyn was where it all started, or at least where the spark was lit in the explosion that was known as disco, which swept through every borough in New York City, then every city in America, and then – helped in no small part by the 1977 movie *Saturday Night Fever* which had its inspiration back in Brooklyn – every country in the world.

According to some, the craze really started in black gay clubs in Manhattan, then spread through the outer New York boroughs, touching every ethnic group from Puerto Ricans and other Latinos in the Bronx and Spanish Harlem, to blacks in Harlem and Queens, to Italians (as with John Travolta's Tony Manero character in *Saturday Night Fever*) in Brooklyn.

In fact, it was a specific Brooklyn club, the 2001 Odyssey in Bay Ridge, that was the actual inspiration for the writer Nik Cohn, upon whose story the eventual movie was based. He later recalled his first visit to the club in the winter of 1975: 'We were in a dead land. There were auto shops, locked and barred; transmission specialists; alignment centres. There was the Crazy Country Club, which advertised 'warm beer and lousy food'. And then there was, at the far end of a deserted block, a small patch of red neon light.'

Musically, disco was in part a development of the way black soul music had moved in the early seventies. The Memphis-based gospel-tinged Stax sound of Otis Redding, Wilson Pickett and such, the sweet soul soundtrack of the sixties, had given way to the smoother 'Philadelphia sound', masterminded by the songwriting-production team of Kenny Gamble and Leon Huff. Their Philadelphia International label would dominate soul through to the middle of the 1970s with artists like Teddy Pendergrass, the O'Jays and Harold Melvin and the Bluenotes topping both the black music (R & B) and mainstream charts.

It involved a mainstream-friendly 'crossover' style often adorned with lush string sections, and even the hard-edged funk legacy of Sly and the Family Stone was dissipated in this process. R & B outfits like Kool and the Gang and the Ohio Players were early examples of the disco approach, with simple but very danceable singles making the crossover from black to white markets with ease. As a harbinger of things to come, two bands from Brooklyn, BT Express and Brass Construction, added strings and horns to this simple dance formula, and for certain record companies – and a host of club DJs – there was no going back.

Like all dance music, disco had its roots in the rhythm section, but it was its social and commercial ramifications that made it much more than just another ballroom craze. The very name was in reference to a venue rather than a sound. Right through the rock 'n' roll era and indeed earlier, club audiences had danced to records, but usually during the interval between live acts. People had always danced to jukeboxes in bars and juke-joints of course, but that hadn't involved paying for the privilege, except the coin in the slot. That changed with the French *discothequè* (some credit the term to film director Roger Vadim who named it after *cinemathequè*, or cinema club), a club specifically geared to dancing to records with no live music.

Indeed, the first manifestations of 'discos' in the USA in the sixties were usually sleazy dance joints where scantily clad dancers would bump and grind in cages. But soon the mechanisation of having a record deck instead of a band met with the increasing studio-orientation of the soul-plus-horns-plus-strings developments in R & B, and the audience took over from the (now absent) band as the centre of attention.

199

Disco appealed to the narcissistic in its audience, and also the overtly exhibitionist, insofar as the dancers were the performers. So in its inception seventies disco proper was often the province of the gay community in the big cities, and also of young urban blacks (who often found the musician-less venues easier on cover charges) – two ghettoised groups finding a way through disco into the social mainstream. Disco clubs evolved as places to live out a fantasy that took you far away from the preoccupations of everyday life. This was borne out in the dress code – glittery, shiny, sprayed-on and dazzling – and in the environment – futuristic and fantastical with dry ice, strobes and flashing lights beneath your feet. You could arrive at the disco and forget about life in the world outside.

Working-class white youth soon cottoned on to disco for the same reasons (and because the records were now making the national charts), and the *Saturday Night Fever* scenario was complete. Travolta's character wasn't gay or black, but a macho working-class white kid from Brooklyn – like dancehall heroes through the ages, basically there to make out with girls.

Disco as a cutting-edge fashion was epitomised in New York's Studio 54 club, opened on 26 April 1977, where a star-studded glitterati of trendy society gathered to boogie the night away. Everyone from Andy Warhol to Liza Minnelli, Debbie Harry to Mick Jagger would be on its prestigious VIP list, while ordinary mortals would queue for hours, hoping to get in despite its notoriously draconian door policy – a long way from the world of Tony Manero in *Saturday Night Fever* released the same year, and the back-street Brooklyn club that had inspired the movie in the first place.

Despite, or maybe because of, its ubiquitous presence on the late-Seventies music scene, by the end of the decade disco suffered a spectacular backlash, typified by the burning of thousands of disco records in a Chicago baseball park in 1979.

ELVIS IS STILL IN THE BUILDING

NASHVILLE, 1977

The famous phrase 'Elvis has left the building' originated during his barnstorming stage shows of the seventies, telling the cheering audience, unwilling to move from their seats, that there would be no more encores – the star had left for the night. Then after he died, it became a catch phrase to confirm that – despite any rumours to the contrary – the King of Rock 'n' Roll had indeed departed once and for all. But it certainly didn't ring true everywhere.

During the fifties, the Nashville recording studios of RCA Records were located on the first floor of a building on McGavock Street that was owned by the Methodist TV, Radio and Film Commission. It was there that Elvis Presley made his debut recordings for the company on 10 January 1956; three tracks (with two more following the next day) that included his first ground-breaking international hit 'Heartbreak Hotel'.

After RCA moved to other, bigger quarters in 1957, the building – just off what is now known as Music Row – became a TV production facility, with studios that were used in the main to produce music and music-related programmes. An audio booth and studio lighting panel occupied the space where Elvis once recorded some of his most historic sides and it was here that strange happenings were reported by members of the studio crew after Presley died in 1977. Apparently, every time Elvis's name was mentioned during a show's production, something strange would happen. Lights would fail, ladders and other equipment would fall over and unexplained noises would suddenly be heard through the sound system. Contrary to the stories circulating that Elvis was alive and well, living in secret somewhere, the weird manifestations in Nashville suggested he was indeed deceased – but still in the building.

WRITTEN IN BLOOD

DEPEW, NEW YORK STATE, 1977

The cartoon-like image of seventies glam-rock stadium rockers Kiss drew upon comic book superheroes almost as much as on the music itself. It wasn't surprising, therefore, when Marvel Comics decided to feature them in an actual comic book of their own.

Someone at Marvel then came up with a marketing gimmick for the first edition that was original to say the least – to put real blood in the ink – the band's blood. The group agreed to the idea with no hesitation, and after having their blood drawn backstage at a gig were flown up to the printing works in Depew, New York, where Marvel produced its world-famous comics. There the band members were photographed adding their vials of donated blood to a barrel of red ink.

A notary public duly certified the authenticity of the entire process, and the notarised document was made available as the 'Kiss comic book contract', and read:

'This is to certify that Kiss members, Gene Simmons, Ace Frehley, Paul Stanley and Peter Criss, have each donated blood which is being collectively mixed with the red ink to be used for the first issue of the Marvel/Kiss comics. The blood was extracted on 21 February 1977 at Nassau Coliseum and has been under guarded refrigeration until this day when it was delivered to the Borden Ink plant in Depew, New York.'

FILTHY PUNKS CLEAN UP

LONDON, 1977

The story of rock music is awash with tales of record companies exploiting musicians and singers, some of the greatest names in music having signed to deals that were a rip-off from start to finish. So the monetary manoeuvrings of the Sex Pistols vis-à-vis the record industry establishment came as a breath of fresh air in the late seventies, when Johnny Rotten and his punk pals turned the tables.

British punk exploded onto the front pages of the British tabloid press when the Pistols famously uttered four-letter expletives in a prime-time TV interview conducted by Bill Grundy on 1 December 1976. But despite (or possibly because of) headlines like, THE FILTH AND THE FURY in the next morning's papers, the band managed to clean up on their notoriety without playing or recording a note of music.

In the wake of the uproar caused by the TV appearance, gigs were cancelled across the country and in January 1977 the band were sacked by their label EMI, who they'd signed with the previous October. However they did get to keep the £40,000 advance that came with the now-defunct contract. Amid more (well-organised) media frenzy that accompanied their every move, they signed with A&M Records on 10 March for an advance of £75,000, only to be dropped by the label just six days later without releasing a single record. Then in May 1977 they put their marks on the dotted line in yet another contract, this time with Virgin Records, for which they received an advance of £15,000. This brought their advances to a then-staggering £130,000, largely accrued through manager Malcolm McLaren's well co-ordinated wheeling and dealing. In the sorry saga of rock 'n' roll exploitation, for once the boot was very firmly, albeit briefly, on the other foot.

TIE THAT KANGAROO DOWN

AUSTRALIA, 1970s

One of the strangest on-tour tales of all time concerns Jerry Lee Lewis on an Australian concert trek that took him across part of that country's vast outback.

It seems the piano-pumping rock 'n' roll legend shouted to his driver to stop after he'd spied a kangaroo in some trees by the roadside. Getting out to investigate, Jerry Lee concluded that the animal, leaning lifelessly against a tree, was in fact dead. He called his roadie over, realising this was a photo opportunity not to be missed.

The two men struggled with the dead weight of the creature as they 'dressed' it in the roadie's tour jacket, Jerry Lee then posing proudly for a photograph.

The 'roo wasn't dead however, the camera flash waking it up from a deep slumber. The startled creature leaped into the bush, never to be seen by the equally surprised rock 'n' rollers again.

So it was, if the story is to be believed, that a wild kangaroo hopped around the Australian outback wearing a silk bomber jacket with 'Jerry Lee Lewis World Tour' emblazoned on the back.

ELVIS LIVES!

MEMPHIS, 1977

Ever since the King of Rock 'n' Roll died at his Graceland mansion on 16 August 1977, rumours, myths and conspiracy theories have abounded purporting that Elvis still lives.

Right after his passing, the story emerged that the superstar had faked his own death in order to escape the pressure of fame, with which he had become bored, disillusioned and too physically tired.

Part 'proof' of this was given that Elvis's name was misspelled on his gravestone, as the traditional 'Aaron' rather than 'Aron' as his name was actually spelled (to match that of his still-born twin brother Jesse Garon). And just hours after Elvis's death was announced, so the story went, a man by the name of Jon Burrows (which was Elvis's travelling alias) purchased a one-way ticket with cash to Buenos Aires. His manager Colonel Tom Parker was claimed to be in on the scam. He was really a Dutch illegal immigrant named Andreas van Kuijk; his entire identity was falsified, and it's proposed that he could have easily done the same for Elvis.

A variation on Parker's involvement in his client's hoax was that he would have been happy to see him 'out of the way' as he had a deal already lined up with RCA records to repackage and promote all Elvis's back catalogue of material, the sales of which would be boosted enormously by the King's demise.

Since then, of course, 'sightings' of the clandestine rock star have proliferated all over the world, in locations as varied as a supermarket in Texas to the Brandenburg Gate in Berlin (where it was claimed he was with his ex-wife Priscilla). One shoe-shop assistant in Hull, England, claimed Elvis came into the shop in 1998, asking for something in blue suede (naturally), while someone in 2005 claimed to have seen him in Macy's department store in New York City – apparently he was fat with a beard, and wearing a hat, but unmistakably Elvis.

One of the most exotic of the hundreds of sightings reported over the years has been in a temple to Hindu god Shiva in New Delhi, while at a more mundane level scores of people have sighted the reclusive ex-rocker in petrol stations, shopping malls and – predictably – hamburger joints. And, of course, we'll always remember Kirsty MacColl's wonderful single released in 1981, 'There's A Guy Works Down The Chip Shop Swears He's Elvis'.

THE WILD LIFE AND SAD DEATH OF MOON THE LOON

LONDON, 1978

No collection of outrageous rock 'n' roll stories would be complete without reference to the Who drummer Keith Moon, whose nickname 'Moon the Loon' was as well deserved as his hell-raising exploits were many.

Moon was notorious for wrecking cars, homes, hotel rooms and even restaurants – it managed to get the Who plenty of free front-page publicity, while fully ensconcing his reputation as *the* lunatic British rock star. It was once estimated that the total damage wreaked by Moon around the world over a span of fourteen years was valued at about a quarter of a million pounds.

Moon quickly gained a reputation as being highly destructive after wrecking his own drum kits on stage. In the mayhem he wreaked in hotels, for instance, he would often throw furniture and TV sets out of high windows and destroy the plumbing with firecrackers. While he never actually drove a car into a swimming pool – that was a myth he perpetuated himself, saying he drove a Lincoln into a Holiday Inn swimming pool for his 21st birthday – it's not hard to imagine how such a story originated.

In 1969 Moon was brought before the High Court of London on charges of vehicular manslaughter. The charges were filed to determine Moon's role in the death of his bodyguard, Cornelius 'Neil' Boland, who was accidentally crushed under the wheels of Moon's pink Rolls-Royce.

Although Boland's death was ruled an accident and Moon was subsequently acquitted of any wrongdoing, those close to him said the drummer was haunted by the accident for the rest of his life.

Moon had moved to America by 1975, and bought a beachside house at Malibu, next door to the movie superstar Steve McQueen. The Hollywood idol valued his privacy, not to mention a bit of peace and quiet, so the mad Englishman was an unsuitable neighbour from the start. After complaining to the police a few times, McQueen built a high wall between the properties. Moon, not to be outdone, built a ramp and bought a motorbike, on which he intended to drive over the wall in the fashion McQueen had raced a bike in the famous scene in *The Great Escape*. Whether he ever tried the feat isn't clear, but at one stage he did knock on his neighbour's door dressed as Hitler, and when a startled McQueen opened it, Moon got down on all fours and bit the actor's dog.

On 6 September 1978 Moon attended a party thrown by Paul McCartney in honour of the movie *The Buddy Holly Story*. It would be his last night out. Sometime in the late afternoon of 7 September, Keith John Moon died in Flat 12, 9 Curzon Place, in London. Coincidentally, it was the same flat that Mama Cass had died in some years before. The flat was on loan to Keith from musician friend Harry Nilsson. Following the loss of a second friend in the building, a distraught Nilsson could not face returning there and subsequently sold the flat to Pete Townshend.

After years of illicit drug-taking, it was somewhat ironic that the prescription drug Heminevrin, prescribed to wean Keith off alcohol, would be the substance that killed him. A postmortem confirmed there were 32 tablets in his system at the time, 26 of which were undissolved.

The conspiracy theorists tell us that he was too experienced a drug user to have accidentally overdosed, that his death was in fact a suicide. Some, including John Entwistle, believe Moon choked to death, that his muscles were just too relaxed to vomit. Most people, however, don't buy the suicide theory, citing Keith's love of life and the fact that he never thought much about even *what* he was taking, let alone how *much* – this was, after all, the same person who gulped down a horse tranquilliser that put him out for two whole days!

THE SAGA OF SID 'N' NANCY

NEW YORK CITY, 1978

The subject of a 1986 feature film (Alex Cox's *Sid and Nancy*), the story of Sid Vicious and Nancy Spungen has been romanticised as the Bonnie and Clyde saga of rock 'n' roll. But in reality, the pair were rock disasters waiting to happen – their coming together just made the inevitable more immediate.

Sid Vicious – real name John Simon Ritchie – had joined the Sex Pistols in 1977 as a replacement for the band's original bass player Glen Matlock. Even though he could hardly play a note, Vicious filled the bill as far as the Pistols' largely contrived 'outrageous' image was concerned. The problem with Sid was, he seemed to seriously believe it was all for real.

He lived the life of the nihilistic rocker hell-bent on self-destruction, rather than just acting it out. The twenty-year-old spat, swore, kicked and punched his way into rock 'n' roll mythology, and – not long after the demise of the Sex Pistols – his end was even more spectacularly violent and debauched than any headline writer could have wished for. It was an end that began to take shape as soon as he got involved with peroxide-haired groupie Nancy Spungen in 1978.

Raised in the neat suburbs of Philadelphia, Spungen had dropped out of the University of Colorado to move to New York City where she worked as a go-go dancer. She soon became a notorious groupie, apparently counting among her 'conquests' Keith Richards, New York proto-punk Richard Hell and Jerry Nolan of the New York Dolls. It was through Nolan that she was reputed to have been introduced to heroin and, by the time she met Sid, had acquired a serious habit. In fact, some sources claim she had the unenviable reputation of having introduced the drug to the UK punk scene when she travelled to England in 1978.

Cynics would say that Sid and Nancy deserved each other, others felt they were their own worst enemies, and together even more so. Sex Pistols vocalist Johnny Rotten would describe Spungen as 'like the Titanic looking for an iceberg'. Whatever, Nancy certainly found her match in the death-wish stakes when she met Sid.

Sid too was on heroin – whether he was initiated in its use by Nancy isn't exactly clear – and it seems almost certain that their mutual addiction led directly to Nancy being found murdered in New York's Chelsea Hotel on the night of 12 October 1978. The police had been called to the hotel after receiving a call from Vicious confessing to his girlfriend's murder. Her body was in the bathroom, with blood everywhere from a stab wound in her side.

According to Sid's account of events, he and Nancy had tried to buy some heroin but the dealer could only supply them with tranquillisers, which they took anyway. But the downers only made Sid's desperation for a fix even worse, and he apparently started banging on the doors of other rooms in the hotel, demanding some hard drugs. A member of staff was called to calm him down, and in the ensuing fight, Sid's nose was broken by a single punch from the hotel concierge.

Returning to his room, the punk star got into an argument with an agitated Nancy, still aching for a fix, and she slapped him on his already sore nose. In temper the ex-Sex Pistol stabbed the girl in the side with a hunting knife – which, it was later learned, she had bought him as a present just the previous day.

It's here that the Vicious version gets a little hard to believe. He would claim that they kissed and made up, not thinking the stab wound was serious! He then went out to get some methadone (he was actually on a heroin withdrawal programme at the time) from the neighbourhood clinic, returning to find Nancy not around. After falling asleep on the bed, thinking his girlfriend had gone out, when he awoke to go to the bathroom he found her there, covered in blood in her black lace underwear.

Whether he slayed her in a drug-induced stupor that he subsequently forgot, or made up a half-hearted lie, the fact that he confessed makes his guilt seem pretty certain. But the violent death of Nancy Spungen was just the beginning of the sorry end of Sid Vicious.

After his arrest he spent some days in prison at Riker's Island, where he was taunted and apparently raped by fellow inmates, who didn't take kindly to the 'tough punk' celebrity in their midst. He was also still suffering the 'cold turkey' of heroin withdrawal, so was more than relieved when the Pistols' manager Malcolm McLaren raised the $50,000 bail money for his temporary release.

But Sid was still plummeting to self-annihilation. After being released too late to make it to Nancy's funeral, he mutilated himself with a broken bottle and blunt razor. His near-suicide resulted in his incarceration at the Bellevue psychiatric hospital in New York; upon his release a few days later, he was back in trouble almost immediately.

He managed to get into a fight in a club, with punk vocalist Patti Smith's brother Todd, after he'd tried to chat up his girlfriend. Breaking a bottle in Smith's face, Sid Vicious was soon behind bars, a guest of the NYPD once again.

After three months in jail, Sid was released to the presumed 'safety' of his mother Anne, but she was no stranger to drugs, and to save him from getting busted for scoring heroin she went and acquired it for her son herself. The stuff Sid's mum got hold of was almost a hundred per cent pure, and Sid predictably OD'd – with fatal consequences. It was never firmly established whether his death was actually suicide or accidental.

The final, rather poignant episode in the Sid and Nancy saga was when his mother dearest got back to London with an urn containing her cremated son's ashes. According to what may be just another rock 'n' roll myth, she dropped the urn as she disembarked at Heathrow Airport – the ashes scattering over the tarmac and blown in every direction as the high-powered jets roared by. It was perhaps a fitting end for a young man whose whole career in rock music seemed to be driven by a nihilistic urge, matched only by that of his equally doomed lover Nancy.

THE DEATH OF DISCO

CHICAGO, 1979

There have been a number of disc-trashing incidents throughout the history of rock music, starting most famously with the destruction of Elvis records by DJs across the American South when 'the Pelvis' first made national headlines with his gyrating stage act. Back in those mid-fifties days, of course, it was originally a case of smashing the discs when they were 10-inch 78s made of brittle shellac – something that couldn't be done once the 'unbreakable' vinyl 45s had taken over. From then on it was down to burning the offending platters, and there were rock 'n' roll bonfires a-plenty through the rest of the decade.

Likewise with the Beatles in the sixties, especially after John Lennon made his infamous 'We're more popular than Jesus' statement, the pop pyres were built high and burned brightly across America.

But the greatest musical conflagration of all time came in the heated backlash against the dominance of disco in the seventies. By the end of the decade, many music lovers were totally fed up with the glitter and glam of the disco scene, combined with the vacuous nature of much of the music.

The 'Disco Sucks' movement, led by the Chicago DJ Steve Dahl, was dedicated to pushing disco out of venues and off radio playlists in favour of rock music. Dahl's missionary zeal reached its peak on the night of 12 July 1979, when he invited listeners to bring their disco records to Comiskey Park, home

216

of the Chicago White Sox baseball team, and take part in a 'Disco Demolition' event.

Thousands of people turned up, and during the break in a double-header ball game between the White Sox and Detroit Tigers, a hundred thousand records were piled high and blown up with dynamite – to the ecstatic cheers of the rock fans – with Dahl leading the way by destroying hundreds of *Saturday Night Fever* soundtrack albums.

Unfortunately a mini riot broke out as fans rushed on to the field, and the home side White Sox had to forfeit the second game. But Dahl and his disco-haters had made their point, and the campaign was credited with speeding up the demise of disco as a ubiquitous pop trend.

TAPE THAT

LONDON, 1980

When the Sex Pistols finally called it a day at the end of the seventies, their manager Malcolm McLaren followed up that project with an equally audacious idea – but one that, in retrospect, was outmoded almost as soon as it got off the ground.

The new group of hopefuls that the 'pop Svengali' put together was called Bow Wow Wow, and their gimmick was that their first single was only available in a cassette-tape format. The group consisted of ex-members of Adam and the Ants fronted by a half-Burmese fifteen-year-old called Annabella Lwin, and their single – 'C30, C60, C90, Go' – was, predictably, a paean to the illegal home taping of music off the radio.

This was clearly against the better instincts of the record company EMI, given that the industry was at the time campaigning against home taping, as it was causing falling record sales. The single eventually made it into the UK Top Forty in 1980, but only when it was subsequently issued on disc. Another tape-only release, 'Your Cassette Pet', came at Christmas 1980, another commercial risk given that this was long before the late-eighties boom in 'cassingles'.

McLaren had discovered Lwin singing in a dry-cleaning shop, and invited her to join the group against the wishes of her mother, who was even more outraged when the group's first album – this time on RCA – appeared. The cover photo, loosely based on Edouard Manet's painting *Le Déjeuner sur l'herbe*, featured her daughter posing nude with the other (fully

218

clothed) members of the group. The album – neatly titled *See Jungle! See Jungle! Go Join Your Gang! Yeah, City All Over! Go Ape Crazy!* – made it into the LP chart, followed by minor hits in 1981. The following year they were in the Top Ten with their singles 'Go Wild In The Country' and 'I Want Candy', and again the album list with *I Want Candy*, but internal wrangles saw them break up in 1983.

Typically of McLaren projects, Bow Wow Wow attempted both to create and exploit a trend at the same time, but in his prediction that cassette records and home taping were going to take over the recording business, McLaren was clearly mistaken. The nubile image of Annabella surfaced again in the nineties with a single 'Car Sex' but it flopped, after which she retired from music and became a Buddhist.

THE ALTER EGO OF JOHN
LENNON'S KILLER

NEW YORK CITY, 1980

When, on the night of 8 December 1980, John Lennon was shot and killed outside the entrance of the Dakota Building where he lived in New York, his killer Mark Chapman secured for himself the kind of fame he would never otherwise have achieved. Many assumed that the desire for such notoriety on the part of the apparent 'loner' was the sum total of his motivation. As a self-evident Lennon fan (he'd asked the ex-Beatle for his autograph earlier in the day), it seemed obvious that he identified with his hero to such a degree that he sought to achieve the same kind of celebrity through destroying him.

But it was soon to transpire that the prime inspiration for the disturbed young man's homicide was in fact Holden Caulfield, the fictional juvenile protagonist of J D Salinger's seminal 1951 novel *Catcher in the Rye*. Described as 'a Huckleberry Finn of the post-World War II generation', in the book Holden runs away from his small-town prep school to have numerous adventures in New York. Acutely aware of all the 'phoniness' he finds in people around him, his self-narrated story in a semi-cynical, part-naïve style struck a chord with a huge section of young readers in the fifties, and helped pave the way for the 'drop-out' philosophy of teenagers in the sixties.

By killing Lennon, who he would later refer to as just 'an image on a screen', Chapman was able to include the star in an intricate fantasy that determined his life. To justify the murder, Chapman would transform himself in his mind to the Salinger character, this act making him (as he saw it) the 'Catcher in the Rye' of his generation.

In his in-depth study of what lay behind Mark Chapman's actions that tragic night (entitled *Let Me Take You Down*), writer Jack Jones tells how Chapman would later confess to being taken by surprise after firing the fatal shots, when Lennon, instead of collapsing at his feet as he'd expected, staggered up five or six steps and crashed through a glass door into the foyer of the Dakota. The killer had anticipated a 'rebirth' as Holden Caulfield, with the dead body of his (former) hero a catalyst in the metamorphosis.

But it was not until he had been incarcerated in jail on Rikers Island for two months that Mark Chapman 'became' the Catcher in the Rye, after intensive sessions with defence lawyers and psychiatrists. He gradually descended into what psychologists call a 'fictive personality', a self-created bizarre version of Holden Caulfield.

According to a University of California psychologist, Jay Martin, Holden Caulfield – along with Elvis Presley, Marilyn Monroe, Batman, Superman and others – was a frequent alter ego in cases like Chapman's, someone lacking a personality of their own. 'A fictional character is unchangeable and safe. It gives a guarantee of a hold upon reality and has stories about it that can be imitated,' said Martin in his book *Who Am I This Time? Uncovering the Fictive Personality*.

Martin felt that *The Catcher in the Rye* appeals particularly to depressed young adults who, like Chapman, suffered psychological trauma in childhood or adolescence that impaired their ability to function in the adult world. 'People who read *The Catcher in the Rye* twenty or thirty years ago don't tend to remember how depressed and psychically injured Holden Caulfield is. But if you go back and read the book, it's very apparent how wounded and how depressed he is,' Martin writes.

Chapman's assumption of the Caulfield persona wasn't sufficient for a plea of insanity on the part of his defence lawyers however and, according to Martin, fictive personas are also often common features of a healthy personality. Chapman was clearly a self-deluding loner, and deceitful to others, but knowingly so. He was no schizophrenic; he *self-consciously* 'created' his alter ego, just as surely as his murder of Lennon was coldly planned, for whatever reason.

Mark Chapman was sentenced to life imprisonment, with no parole until 2000. In October of that year, his first parole application was rejected, and he's still serving time in the Attica State Prison.

EASY RIDERS: THE M&M CLAUSE

US, 1980s

Along with trashed hotel rooms and armies of groupies, one of the most conspicuous areas of rock-star excess is in the contract rider – the food, drink and other 'necessities' requested backstage at a gig.

It seems the Beatles were the first touring act with enough drawing power to make demands of this kind (with the possible exception of Elvis back in the fifties), but their requirements were extremely modest by the standards of bands that followed their example. Apparently all they asked for backstage at the legendary Shea Stadium concert in 1965 was a black-and-white television set and a crate of Coca-Cola.

The Rolling Stones, on the other hand, were (and still are) famous for riders that run to several dozen pages, with highly detailed specifications for the serving of gourmet food and drink after the show.

Even more outrageous requests have come from everyone from Iggy Pop (who once asked for seven dwarves!) to Prince (one of whose demands includes having a physician on hand before every show to inject him with a Vitamin B12 shot).

Marilyn Manson asks that every room he enters be chilled to a deathly freeze with air-conditioning on full, a never-ending supply of Coca-Cola and a bottomless bucket of ice. And it doesn't stop there – the shock-horror rocker also demands gummi bears, mini chocolates, Doritos, soya milk, assorted flavours of sweetened Kool Aid, Hanson's cherry vanilla soda and microwave popcorn before and after a show.

Divas can't come more demanding than Mariah Carey, who has been known to ask for bunny rabbits, puppies and kittens to keep her company backstage – not to mention the best champagne, a box of bendy straws to sip it with, and (she wasn't joking) an attendant to dispose of her used chewing gum!

But Jennifer Lopez certainly vies with Mariah in the 'I won't go on unless I have it' stakes. She once demanded a trailer to herself, furnished all in white with flowers, tablecloths, drapes, candles, couches, a VCR and CD player, plus 43 music CDs of her own choice. Rumour has it she also demands that her coffee is only to be stirred anti-clockwise!

But the most celebrated rider of all is the request on the part of heavy-metal merchants Van Halen for a bowl of M&M chocolates with all the brown ones removed. It wasn't, however, an utterly extravagant demand for no good purpose other than to satisfy the musicians' egos that they could make the demand. The idea of putting the clause in was that if a promoter ignored the 'no brown ones' request, it suggested he or she hadn't read the rest of the small print either, which could have disastrous or even fatal consequences.

Lead vocalist with the group, David Lee Roth, spelled out their reasoning in his autobiography: 'The contract rider read like a version of the Chinese Yellow Pages because there was so much equipment, and so many human beings to make it function. So just as a little test, in the technical aspect of the rider, it would say "Article 148: There will be fifteen amperage voltage sockets at twenty-foot spaces, evenly, providing nineteen amperes . . ." That kind of thing. And article number 126, in the middle of nowhere, was: "There will be no brown M&M's in the backstage area, upon pain of forfeiture of the show, with full compensation."

It's all a long way from when Ringo really hoped there might be some whisky to go with that crate of Coca-Cola!

COLLINS FANS IN THE AIR

LONDON, 1981

One of the most bizarre stories in rock 'n' roll folklore came out of the misinterpretation of lyrics by fans of Phil Collins. The song in question was his 1981 UK Top Five hit 'In The Air Tonight', his first chart smash after leaving the band Genesis and going solo that same year.

Although the song was apparently a comment on Collins's failed marriage, the fans took two lines literally. 'Well, if you told me you were drowning / I would not lend a hand' was thought to refer to Collins having witnessed the drowning of a real-life friend from afar, where a stranger who was closer to the drowning man offered no assistance.

From there on in, the myth took on further embellishments. Phil Collins is supposed to have tracked the man down, given him a free ticket to one of his concerts, then debuted the song with a spotlight trained on the offender. Two subsequent additions to the story also began to circulate, one that the negligent man was then arrested as a result of Collins tracking him down, the other that the guilt-ridden individual, full of remorse following the concert exposé, committed suicide.

ROCK'S FORGOTTEN SUPERSTAR

HARLINGEN, TEXAS, 1981

Kiss-curled rock pioneer Bill Haley pre-empted Elvis Presley by more than a year in the pop charts, and represented the true breakthrough of rock 'n' roll. He had his first Top Twenty hits in 1954 – 'Dim Dim The Lights' and 'Shake Rattle And Roll' – and six more in 1955, including 'Rock Around the Clock.

When 'Rock Around The Clock' was featured in the 'juvenile delinquent' movie *The Blackboard Jungle* in 1955, teenagers rioted in cinemas across Britain and America, and the mayhem was repeated with the release of the movie *Rock Around The Clock* in 1956. Bill's days in the charts were numbered, however, after the far sexier Elvis assumed the crown of King of Rock 'n' Roll, but Bill and his band the Comets continued to play around the world.

In 1955, Bill Haley and the Comets were reported to have earned over half a million dollars from live appearances alone – a phenomenal sum in those days. Prior to Haley's death in 1981, over a hundred musicians had passed through the Comets, who gigged more or less nonstop until ill health incapacitated Bill in 1980. Subsequently 'Rock Around The Clock' went on to be the third-biggest-selling single of all time, with sales totalling thirty million worldwide.

Bill Haley died aged 55 from a heart attack on 9 February 1981 at his home in Harlingen, Texas. Apparently he died penniless, a heavy drinker riddled with paranoia, living in his garage, the walls of which he'd painted black. Reports at the time of his death claimed that none of his neighbours actually knew that the reclusive man who'd just died was actually rock 'n' roll's first great superstar.

OZZY OSBOURNE AND THAT BAT

DES MOINES, IOWA, 1982

The incident involving Ozzy Osbourne biting the head off a live bat is as closely associated with the singer's wild image as that of comedian Freddie Starr eating someone's hamster. Whether the Starr episode actually happened doesn't concern us here, but the Osbourne legend has to be laid to rest once and for all – sorry Oz fans, but it simply isn't true.

Certainly there have been some famous outrages perpetuated by the ex-Black Sabbath singer, particularly in the early days of his solo career. He was indeed arrested in Texas for relieving himself on that most hallowed of shrines in the Lone Star State – the Alamo; and he *did* bite the head off a live dove in 1980 as he signed his solo contract with Jet Records. However, it wasn't Ozzy who bit the bat; it was the other way round.

In the early 1980s, a regular feature of Ozzy's live shows was at the end, when he threw animal hearts, brains, intestines etc., into the crowd. In 1982, when he was playing a concert in Des Moines, Iowa, a fan reciprocated by throwing a live bat onto the stage. The bat was stunned by the light and Ozzy, thinking the creature was a plastic toy, picked it up and put it in his mouth. The bat, struggling and flapping its wings, bit the heavy-metal idol and he had to be rushed to hospital to be tested for rabies.

Of course, it was a golden publicity opportunity, and Ozzy milked it for all he was worth, encouraging his press reputation as 'the man who bit off more than he can chew', declaring long after the event, 'It took me a lot of water just to down that f****** bat's head, let me tell you. It's still stuck in my f****** throat after all these years!' The legend has stuck too – in 2000 there was even an Ozzy tribute album entitled (after the Stones' *Goat's Head Soup*) *Bat Head Soup*.

THE MANSLAUGHTER OF MARVIN GAYE

LOS ANGELES, 1984

After a career of ups and downs, things were looking good for Motown superstar Marvin Gaye as 1983 began. His latest album *Midnight Love* included 'Sexual Healing', which is one of Gaye's most famous songs and was his final big hit. The hit finally gave Gaye the respect he deserved, as he won two Grammy Awards in February 1983 for the song (Best R & B Male Vocal Performance and Best R & B Instrumental). A couple of months later he embarked on a tour to promote the album; he was plagued by continuing health problems, however, before the tour ended in August 1983.

Gaye's re-found success had pushed him even deeper into the drug addiction and paranoia that had darkened his life in recent years. Throughout the tour he had premonitions that someone was going to kill him, and hired a posse of bodyguards to surround him constantly – he even wore a bulletproof vest. After the tour ended, he attempted to isolate himself from the outside world by moving into his parents' house in Los Angeles, where he threatened to commit suicide several times after numerous bitter arguments with his father, Marvin Gay (the correct family spelling) Sr.

Throughout much of his life, Marvin Sr had had a troubled relationship with his son. He was a pastor in the Hebrew Pentecostal Church, in a suburb of Washington DC, and the church naturally became a focal point for the entire family. His offspring's occupation didn't please him and, from Marvin Jr's childhood days, father and son had a tempestuous relationship. Some close to the family said that from early on the pastor resented the applause his son's singing would receive, adulation that his church sermons never seemed to attract. But despite this religious vocation, he proved perhaps unconventional as a pastor, with a liking for dressing up in women's clothing and a voracious appetite for vodka.

The argument Marvin had with his father on 1 April 1984 however, one day before his 45th birthday, proved one too many. Gaye was shot and killed by the pastor, becoming a famous victim of that rare crime, paternal filicide. According to police reports, Marvin Gaye's last words to his father were 'Nigga, this best be an April Fool's joke!' Relatives claimed that he had purposely pushed his father to the edge so that he could have Marvin Sr kill him instead of having to commit suicide. Pastor Gay was convicted of voluntary manslaughter and given a six-year suspended prison sentence. He died of pneumonia in 1998.

HOT LICKS

LOS ANGELES, 1980s

Big is better – or you would have thought that was the assumption, ever since various male rock stars in the fifties were rumoured to wear a rolled-up newspaper or similar device inside their trousers, to exaggerate nature's endowment. And the notorious 'Chicago plaster caster' groupies of the late sixties only maximised the myth with their personally cast effigies of famous genitalia.

But Gene Simmons, bass guitarist and vocalist with seventies glam rockers Kiss, is probably unique in making his claim to fame the extraordinary length of his tongue. It is a trademark appendage to be sure – when the band in their full cartoon-like make-up were photographed, Simmons invariably stuck it out as far as it would protrude – which was a long, long way. He confessed to never really noticing its length until he was a teenager, saying, 'That's when it came in handy with the girls.'

More outrageous than what Gene might have got up to with his 'special feature' however, was the totally unsubstantiated rumour that spread among fans – that Simmons had actually had a cow's tongue surgically grafted on to his natural one. Ouch!

JACKO'S BID FOR BONES

CALIFORNIA, 1987

The rather extravagantly nicknamed King of Pop, Michael Jackson, has always had a penchant for things exotic and grotesque, clearly demonstrated in his choice of pets at his Neverland Ranch. The epic video for 'Thriller' in 1984 had the singer transformed into a werewolf and a zombie and there are even rumours of his reconstructed nose falling off during a performance.

The superstar seems to have been aiming at both bases in 1987, when it was reported that he had offered $50,000 for the remains of deformed Victorian-era medical patient Joseph Merrick, immortalised by John Hurt (as John Merrick) in David Lynch's 1980 film *The Elephant Man*. But whether Jackson did in fact make the offer or not, he certainly hasn't been able to take ownership of the bones. The organs from the real Elephant Man were kept in jars at the Royal London Hospital until World War II, when they were destroyed in a German air raid. Casts of the unfortunate man's head, an arm and a foot survive, but are not for sale and so will never find their way into Jacko's collection.

THE DARK SIDE OF
EUROPEAN ROCK

EUROPE, 1990s

Of all the many sub-genres of heavy-metal rock, 'death metal' – and the closely related 'black metal' – has produced the most bizarre and disturbing manifestations outside the music itself, particularly in mainland Europe where its association with violence, fascism and satanism have had some horrific results.

The Norwegian group Mayhem, formed in 1984, is considered the pioneer of black metal in Europe. The founder of Mayhem was guitarist Oystein Aarseth (who originally called himself 'Destructor' but later changed his name to 'Euronymous', allegedly meaning 'the prince of death'). The rest of the group was made up of 'Necro Butcher' on bass, vocalist 'Dead', and 'Hellhammer' on drums. One of the trademarks of Mayhem and other Norwegian black-metal groups was the wearing of 'corpse paint', black-and-white make-up designed to create a morbid death-like appearance. Aarseth, who also operated an occult bookstore/record shop in Oslo called Helvete (the Norse word for Hell) that was highly influential upon young fans, was stabbed to death in 1993 aged only 26 by another death-metal rocker, Varg Vikernes, of the group Burzum.

Earlier, the vocalist for Mayhem, Per Yngve Ohlin (aka Dead), had blown his brains out with a shotgun in April 1991, his body being found by Oystein Aarseth. Before the police arrived, Aarseth took pictures of Ohlin's shattered body and collected pieces of his brain and skull. Describing the death of his fellow band member, Aarseth allegedly replied with a complete lack of concern, 'Yeah, Dead killed himself.' Aarseth made necklaces with the skull pieces and cooked some of the brain and apparently ate it, 'so he could claim himself to be a cannibal'. Ohlin, who hated cats and tried to cut them with knives, also saw himself 'as a creature from another world', and had once stabbed Aarseth with a knife.

The death-metal cult in Scandinavia has also been connected with the burning of churches. Since 1992 there have been at least fifty church fires and attempted arson attacks in Norway alone. Roughly a third have a documented connection to the metal rock scene and what the police described as 'Black Metal Satanists'. In fact, Oystein Aarseth's killer Varg Vikernes is strongly suspected of setting the first church alight in 1992 – an ancient building in Fantoft, Norway.

It was also in 1992 that Bard Eithun, the drummer with another Norwegian death-metal band, Emperor, stabbed a homosexual to death for no reason other than the lust of killing. A fellow band member said Eithun had been fascinated with serial killers for a long time. The day after the murder, Eithun participated in a church burning.

Meanwhile, there were roughly a dozen church fires in Germany from late 1993 to early 1997, most having a proven link to black metal and its attendant satanism. The members of the German group Absurd, composed of three high-school students – Hendrik Mobus, Sebastian Schauscheill and Andreas K – murdered a fifteen-year-old classmate in April 1993. The group also called themselves 'Children of Satan', and the band's leader Mobus stated in an interview that, 'We are at the dawn of the New Aeon, when Christendom will perish and a neo-heathen state will arise.'

And in Sweden in 1992, at a Halloween celebration attended by members of death-metal groups Dissection and Abruptum, an elderly man was stabbed repeatedly in the neck by an eighteen-year-old who had been instructed to prove he could kill without compunction. A member of Dissection was also imprisoned for desecrating no less than 250 graves.

Grave desecration seemed even more rampant than church burning among the death-metal fraternity, although the British band Necropolis were convicted of both in 1994. But one of the most horrific instances of metal rockers gone mad was in France in 1996, when a member of the group Funeral, Anthony Mignoni (known as 'Hades') was convicted of desecrating a grave. He and three others exhumed the body of Yvonne Foin, who had been dead twenty years, and placed a cross in the cadaver's heart area.

Another youth that police believe to be associated with Mignoni, David Oberdorf, murdered a priest by stabbing him 33 times with a dagger, carving symbols on the body after the man was dead. He had apparently confronted the priest with the words, 'I am possessed by the demon – I must annihilate men of religion!' Investigators found a collection of death-metal CDs in the teenager's bedroom, and neighbours testified that they had heard 'gnawing music, hard and stressful', blaring from the room. Mignoni later stated that he created the group Funeral, 'to spread my ideas based on the destruction of the Jewish, Christian, and Muslim religions, and on the purity and supremacy of the true Aryan race.' Truly scary stuff.

RAY CHARLES KICKS PORK HABIT

AUCKLAND, NEW ZEALAND, 1991

Soul pioneer and musical legend Ray Charles travelled to most parts of the world in his long career, and incidents on tour over the years were many and varied. In the early days, when he and a good many of his band were heavily into drugs, a lot of the scrapes and crises on the road were directly related to brushes – or near-brushes – with the law. But in latter years, after the singer had famously kicked his heroin habit of the mid-sixties, he ran a strictly drug-free outfit, which made a near-bust by New Zealand authorities even more of a surprise in February 1991, especially when all Ray was carrying was some bacon!

Charles and the band had been booked for a couple of gigs in New Zealand by Australian promoter Glenn Wheatley, who went to meet Ray at the airport in Auckland to supervise things in case there were any problems getting the musicians and entourage through customs. Unfortunately, one of the band members was carrying a very small amount of marijuana in his jacket, and New Zealand, with its strict rules about importing foodstuffs, always has sniffer dogs at points of entry. As Wheatley would put it, 'This time it was more than a packet of biscuits that excited them.'

As soon as the police dogs smelled the drug, one of them just pounced on the guy's crotch, trying to get at what was in his trouser pocket. Ray's manager Joe Adams went crazy – 'Who's in charge here?' – and Wheatley put his hand up. The irate Adams demanded Wheatley get the dog off, while the policeman patiently explained that as the musician was obviously carrying something, they had to 'go through the process'. A customs official was summoned, who confirmed on searching him that the guy was carrying a very small amount of dope, obviously just for his personal use. But the police in New Zealand took a very dim view of this kind of thing, and began talking about having to deport the musician, maybe with the rest of the band. Seeing a crisis looming, an 'international incident' even, Wheatley made a successful effort to calm things down, and got the police to go easy in this instance.

By this time however, more trouble was about to erupt. Ray, it seems, had a habit of eating dried pork rind, and he had in his pocket a little plastic bag of pork rinds. To the dogs he smelled like a bacon rasher, so now they were leaping on the blind singer as well. This time manager Adams went berserk, shouting at Wheatley, 'Get that dog off Mr Charles, now!'

One minute Ray Charles was simply confused, listening to the hubbub going on around him with the errant musician, police and customs folk, the next he had the dogs crawling all over him. Again, the promoter had to dampen some riled individuals, this time not just the authorities but Charles himself, and his testy manager who started talking about pulling out of the gig: 'We all calmed everything down, and I had to sit down and negotiate through this very carefully, signing a guarantee that these people wouldn't be doing any more substances, and there would be good behaviour while they were in New Zealand.' The next time they entered the country, it's a fair guess that Ray Charles would be as wary about carrying pork as pot when the band passed through customs.

THE WORLD'S QUIETEST
ROCK BAND

NEW YORK CITY, 1992

There have been plenty of contenders for the title of the loudest rock 'n' roll band in the world, but there's a band in New York City that's proud to bill itself as playing 'the quietest rock 'n' roll ever made'.

Back in 1964, an acoustics expert from New South Wales University measured the noise level during a Beatles' concert at 112 decibels. But the Beatles then played through what would now be considered very modest equipment, so it's fair to assume that the excruciating volume was produced by screaming fans!

Deep Purple held the title of 'World's Loudest Rock Band' in the 1975 *Guinness Book of World Records*, but it only lasted for a year; in 1976, the Who were cited as the loudest ever, reaching 120 decibels during a show in England, and heavy metal band Motorhead held the title for a five-year run before being eventually outgunned by AC/DC.

Metal monsters Manowar set the record at an ear-splitting 129.5 decibels during a tour of Britain in 1984. Through their ten tons of amplifiers and speakers they even surpassed that at a German date in 1994, with bassist Joey DeMaio registering an awesome 130.7 – just ten less decibels than a Boeing 747 produces on take-off.

In sharp contrast to such bombastic brain battering, there's the aforementioned 'quietest rock 'n' roll' outfit', a New York duo called Drink Me whose unique sound consists of guitars, ukuleles and the rhythmic rubbing of a Fanta soda bottle. Mark Amft sings lead vocals and alternates playing the Fanta bottle (which is ridged, and played by scraping up and down with a stick, like a South American guiro), ukulele, slide guitar, accordion, tambourine and kazoo. Wynne Evans plays guitar and sings harmonies.

They started out in 1986 with Amft on drums and Evans on electric guitar, but moved to a totally acoustic approach, and even on their 1992 debut album, *Drink Me*, the addition of trumpet, trombone and mandolin still meant the absence of any electrical instruments.

A second album, *Sleep*, and a subsequent EP broadened their sound by including a touch of electric bass guitar and Farfisa organ to fill out some songs, but with such exotica as a bowed xylophone and 'Dipsy Doodle corn-chip bag' in the instrumental line-up, Drink Me continued to lay claim to being the quietest band in rock 'n' roll.

PAUL, GEORGE, RINGO . . . AND JOHN

SUSSEX, ENGLAND, 1994

Between the years of 1977 and 1980, John Lennon composed many songs at the piano in his Dakota Building apartment in New York City. One of his songs, 'Free as a Bird', was recorded by Lennon on a cassette-tape machine, but was never finished. Working on *The Beatles Anthology* albums in the early nineties, the remaining Beatles wanted to release several new songs but, of course, wished to include John Lennon. So, in 1994, John's widow Yoko Ono entrusted three of John's recordings to Paul McCartney, George Harrison and Ringo Starr for the first 'Beatles' sessions since 1970. These three were 'Grow Old With Me', 'Real Love' and 'Free As A Bird'.

In March 1994, Paul, George and Ringo went into the studio to add their voices to the old Lennon demo of 'Free As A Bird'. Afterwards, the three surviving Beatles posed for a photo outside the studio. In the instant before the photographer snapped the shutter, a white peacock wandered into the shot.

'That's John,' McCartney said when they saw the pictures, adding later that there was an eerie feeling through the rest of the session that Lennon was 'hanging around . . . we felt that all through the recording'. McCartney also told *Observer Music Monthly* that the group put a backwards recording at the end of the single as a joke, 'to give all those Beatles nuts something to do'. Listening to the finished recording in the studio one night, McCartney claims that in the middle of the otherwise indecipherable garble, the words 'jooohn lennnnon' could clearly be heard.

THE METAL MURDERERS

US, 1990s

Unlike in Europe, where much of the overt crime and violence associated with death metal has been committed by the band members themselves, in the United States it's more often than not been the fans 'inspired' by a particular band that have created murderous mayhem.

As far back as the late sixties, mass-murderer Charles Manson famously claimed that the Beatles' track 'Helter Skelter' drove his homicidal ambition, but it was with metal music in the nineties that freaked-out fans went on the rampage in the name of their particular heavy heroes.

In January 1993, two fifteen-year-old boys mutilated a neighbour's dog; they later told police that their fascination with Florida death-metal band Deicide led them to commit the atrocity. Next, in April 1994, a female employee of a convenience store was brutally murdered, and another woman nearly murdered, by teenagers in Eugene, Oregon. The families of the dead woman sued, claiming that the youths were heavily influenced by the music of Deicide and Cannibal Corpse. The youths had allegedly been listening to Deicide music in a church parking lot shortly before the bloodbath, and one of the killers told the police that he was inspired by Chris Barnes, the lead singer of Cannibal Corpse. The cases were settled out of court, with the record labels paying substantial sums while 'expressly not admitting guilt'.

In July 1995, three teenagers in California – Royce Casey, Jacob Delashmutt and Joseph Fiorella – who were 'fanatical

Slayer fans' and members of a death-metal band called Hatred, murdered fifteen-year-old Elyse Pahler as a satanic sacrifice. Apparently, as Pahler prayed to God and called out for her mother, they stabbed her at least twelve times, leaving her to bleed to death. They were later quoted as saying they chose Pahler because, 'her blonde hair and blue eyes and virginity made her a perfect sacrifice to the devil.'

When the chief investigator asked one of the youths why they committed such a deed, he replied that 'It was to receive power from the devil to help us play the guitar better,' so they could 'play crazier and harder', and, 'go professional'. Two other youngsters associated with the three were convicted of murdering a 75-year-old woman. The murder of Elyse Pahler had been unsolved for months until Casey came forward to the police and guided them to the body. He said he had 'new-found religious beliefs', and was afraid that the others would kill him if he distanced himself from them. Casey told the police that a lyric from the band Slayer warned, 'If you're not with us, you may no longer exist.'

Also in 1995, a Pennsylvania fan of Wisconsin death-metal band, the Electric Hellfire Club, murdered a woman and her young daughter and violated their corpses. The title of the band's 1993 debut album was *Burn, Baby, Burn!* and it depicted a church in flames on the cover, while the lyrics to one of their most popular songs 'Age Of Fire' state: 'Synagogues and churches burning / Can't you see the tide is turning? / How many fires will it take? / Before you realise your god is dead?'

In April 1996, a group of dedicated right-wing death-metal fans that called themselves the Lords of Chaos, went on a crime, arson and murder spree in Fort Myers, Florida. They burned a Baptist church and a large tropical aviary containing a collection of exotic birds. They also burned down a former Coca-Cola bottling plant and then murdered the director of their high-school marching band, blasting him in the face at close range with a shotgun because he had stopped them from vandalising the school the day before. The leader of the group, eighteen-year-old Kevin Foster, was referred to by the others as 'God'. Before being caught by police, the group were making plans to dress up in costumes and then walk through Disney World, shooting any black tourists they came across with silencer-equipped guns.

So notorious were the crimes of this gang that in 1998 they inspired the title of a seminal book on the subject of death metal and its extra-musical influence by Michael Moynihan and Didrik Søderlind – *Lords of Chaos: The Bloody Rise of the Satanic Metal Underground.*

SUICIDE IN NIRVANA

SEATTLE, 1994

As with many deaths of rock 'n' roll superstars, when Nirvana front man Kurt Cobain apparently committed suicide, alternative explanations as to his death were immediately voiced.

The angst-driven songwriter of the Seattle band that spearheaded the 'grunge' movement of the early nineties was rightly considered a spokesman of a generation. Cobain was also a walking disaster waiting to happen in terms of his chronic heroin habit and consequent lifestyle. Being married to singer Courtney Love probably didn't help, as her own history was also fraught with personal traumas.

The 27-year-old singer was found dead in a conservatory above the garage of his Seattle home on 7 April 1994, his head blasted by a shotgun that lay by his side. Also beside the body was his open driver's licence to show his picture for identification as well as a brief suicide note.

It would seem to have been a fairly simple open-and-shut case. Cobain had purchased the gun a short time before at a local gun shop and, even though reports spoke of his head being 'blown off', a police witness later revealed that the blast had damaged his mouth and brain but left much of his face intact. Despite that, however, when the body was discovered two days after Kurt's suicide, it was said to be so badly disfigured as to require fingerprint identification – which was established immediately.

But the conspiracy theories began to flourish as soon as Cobain's death was announced. Some maintained that the singer had faked his own death in order to get away from the increasingly fractious relationship with his wife, others that the two of them had rigged the 'suicide' (with an unknown third party the real victim) so he could escape his downward-plunging lifestyle.

Other rumours, mainly bandied about on Internet sites, claimed Kurt Cobain had actually been murdered – with a mysterious 'hit man' claiming he'd been offered thousands of dollars by 'certain parties' to kill the star. He turned the job down, so the story went, but someone else was then recruited.

Theories as to who did the recruiting to do away with the Nirvana front man varied from the CIA or FBI (for his leading astray the nation's youth?) to record company people with a grudge, and even members of Cobain's own family – including Courtney Love, now his widow, of course. It seems that in the depths of her presumed grief, the Hole singer still couldn't escape the venom of those with an axe to grind about her having married Kurt Cobain in the first place.

A GHOST IN THE MACHINE

MUSCLE SHOALS, ALABAMA, 1995

As well as the Nashville studio that Elvis was said to haunt after his death in 1977, there have been several other examples of musical poltergeists making their presence felt in recording facilities.

In Hartland, Wisconsin, for instance, the Millevolte Recording Studio is bordered by the town cemetery and a historic Native American trading post. Studio owner Vinnie Millevolte claimed that late at night you could sometimes hear doors creaking, someone coming up the stairs or something moving in the kitchen and, in his own words, 'If people aren't scared by them, they seem to get bored and leave.' Millevolte was further convinced of the apparent haunting when a single unexplainable sound, like a heartbeat, was once captured on tape during a recording session.

Actor and singer Billy Bob Thornton has a recording studio in his basement called the Cave, which used to be a speakeasy during the roaring twenties and has secret passages that wind beneath Beverly Hills all the way to the border with West Hollywood. Now, it's a cosy recording studio, built originally by Slash of Velvet Revolver when he, his wife and several snakes lived in the house (which has also been owned by movie magnate Cecil B DeMille, among others). Now the snakes are gone, it serves as Billy Bob's retreat within his home, and has been used by some of the finest talents in rock, blues, pop and country music. Among them have been Slash, the Ventures and the late Warren Zevon – and it's Zevon who

Billy Bob claims is haunting the place, his spirit dwelling in the studio where he recorded his version of Bob Dylan's 'Knocking On Heaven's Door'.

However, it's at the famous 3614 Jackson Highway studios in Muscle Shoals, Alabama, that the most regular sightings have been made of a rock revenant. Famously name-checked by Cher on her 1969 album *3614 Jackson Highway*, the Muscle Shoals (Alabama) Sound Studio, to give it its official title, has played host to scores of great names including Rod Stewart, Paul Simon, Lynyrd Skynyrd, Bob Seger and the Rolling Stones.

One of the studio's regular session players was guitarist Eddie Hinton, who wrote songs and played back-up for scores of famous artists including Wilson Pickett, Arthur Conley, Aretha Franklin, Joe Tex, Solomon Burke, Percy Sledge, the Staple Singers, the Dells, Elvis Presley, the Box Tops, Boz Scaggs and Otis Redding.

Born in June 1944, Hinton played around the South with various groups – one of which was called the Spooks – before becoming one of the first outside musicians to move to the increasingly influential Muscle Shoals scene, where he played lead guitar for Muscle Shoals Sound Rhythm Section from 1967 to 1971.

As well as playing with some of the legends of rock and soul in the studio, and backing R & B greats Wilson Pickett, Percy Sledge and Ted Taylor on tour, Eddie Hinton's songwriting was recognised from his earliest days in Muscle Shoals. His songs have been recorded by artists such as Aretha Franklin, Percy Sledge, Bobby Womack, Cher, Tony Joe White, Gregg Allman, Bonnie Bramlett, Dusty Springfield, Lulu, the Box Tops, the Sweet Inspirations and UB40 (to name but a few!).

Hinton's personal life was less successful, however, and after a traumatic divorce his alcohol and drugs problems got worse, to the extent that he worked less and less, and by the mid-eighties found himself living on the streets of Decatur, Alabama. It was there that he ran into an old friend, John D Wyker; a native of Decatur, he had known Hinton since the early sixties in the University of Alabama drum and bugle corps. Wyker too had seen the downside of the rock 'n' roll lifestyle, so he was sympathetic to Hinton's refusal to take a handout. Eddie was sitting on a bench at the bus stop in front of the Salvation Army, with his clothes and other belongings in an old garbage bag and a small handle-less suitcase.

Wyker arranged for him to go into the studio once again, out of which came a favourably reviewed album *Letters From Mississippi*. Two more albums followed, and after touring Europe it looked like Eddie Hinton's life was on the up again. He even reconciled his relationship with his mother, whom he had not spoken to for some time when his life hit the skids.

But, ironically, the return to the good life began to take its toll and he gained weight and got little exercise. This eventually became his undoing, as a heart condition brought on by his alcoholism came to a head in Birmingham, Alabama, where a heart attack left him dead on 28 July 1995.

Since that time, musicians waiting for their turn at the 3614 Jackson Highway studios (where Eddie enjoyed his greatest successes) have reported seeing an unknown man in a blue suit hanging around the place, never entering or leaving, but just seen wandering about among the recording equipment or up and down corridors – his outfit identical to the one that Eddie Hinton was buried in.

BOB 'N' DAVE

LONDON, 1990s

A famous story that did the rounds in the late nineties involved Bob Dylan and a guy called Dave. Dylan was in London, and decided to call on his friend, the ex-Eurythmics guitarist and producer Dave Stewart. The singer had never been to Stewart's house before, but had the address, which was in the Crouch End district of North London.

Arriving at the house and ringing the doorbell, he was greeted by a woman to whom he announced he'd come to see Dave. 'Dave's just gone out, he'll only be a few minutes,' she replied (or words to that effect) and invited Dylan in, giving him a cup of tea while he waited.

Dylan, however, had managed to get the number wrong on the address, so when Dave (a life-long Bob Dylan fan as it happened) arrived back and his wife/girlfriend said there was a weird guy waiting to see him in the other room, he was amazed to find, sitting in *his* house drinking tea, none other than his idol. Dylan, not surprisingly, was just as dumbfounded, realising this wasn't the Dave he was looking for. Whatever. They both saw the funny side of the mistake and, so the story goes, stayed in touch – after Dave helped Bob find the other Dave of course.

THE MYSTERIOUS DISAPPEARANCE
OF RICHEY EDWARDS

AUST, GLOUCESTERSHIRE, 1995

One of the great mysteries of modern rock music was the disappearance without trace of Richey Edwards – co-lyricist and rhythm guitarist with Welsh indie band, the Manic Street Preachers – in February 1995.

Richey was born in the mining community of Blackwood, Gwent on 22 December 1967 to Sheryl and Graham Edwards, a pair of devout Methodists who ran a hairdresser's on Blackwood High Street. He was a quiet, acne-ridden kid – the archetypal teenage misfit. Though not enamoured with what he had to read at school, he went his own way, and became a huge fan of writers as diverse as George Orwell, Sylvia Plath and Brett Easton Ellis. He also loved music – Echo and the Bunnymen and Public Enemy in particular.

Studying for a Political Science degree at Swansea University, he soon became disenchanted with student life, describing it as, 'Full of people who wanted to sit around and do as little as possible, other than have as much fun as they could. But I never equated university with fun. I thought it was about reading and learning.' That was when he got involved with a bunch of fellow students, the embryo Manics, first of all as their 'roadie', then as their ad hoc PR man (they called him their 'Minister of Information') putting together innumerable press releases for the London-based music papers. It wasn't long before he was playing rhythm guitar as the band's fourth member.

While not a remarkable guitar player by any means ('I can't play guitar very well, but I wanna make the guitar look lethal,' he was once quoted as saying) despite some coaching from lead guitarist/vocalist James Bradfield, Richey began to really make his mark in lyric-writing for the band. His material was often heavy stuff, with thorny, often bleak topics like prostitution, capital punishment and the Holocaust, issues previously considered taboo. His songs became anthems for the marginalised, alienated and dispossessed.

But soon after the band had started to take off in the early nineties, it was apparent that Richey's fertile mind was in a fragile state. He even spawned a slogan, '4Real', which was a grim reference to an infamous incident at a gig at Norwich Arts Centre in May 1991. Challenged at the time by then-*NME* journalist Steve Lamacq to prove the weight of his conviction, Richey carved the term into his arm with a razor. 'When I cut myself I feel so much better,' he would say of his habit. 'All the little things that might have been annoying me suddenly seem so trivial because I'm concentrating on the pain. I'm not a person who can scream and shout so this is my only outlet. It's all done very logically.'

However, by May 1993, his anorexia and alcoholism had reached such a dangerous level that he required professional help; the guitarist spent much of that summer institutionalised in an effort to kick his psychoses, bouncing from an NHS ward in Wales to famous 'celebrity' detox clinic the Priory. Nevertheless, when the delicate subject of his state of mind was raised, Edwards was quick to insist that he would never put his life in danger: 'In terms of the s-word, that does not enter my mind. And it never has done, in terms of an attempt. Because I am stronger than that.'

Then, on the eve of an American tour, Richey Edwards simply disappeared. Most of the details, for what they're worth, have been well documented but there remain few concrete facts and even fewer leads.

The band had begun rehearsing in January 1995 at the House in the Woods studio in Surrey, having just entered into negotiations to write the theme tune for Sylvester Stallone's new film, *Judge Dredd*. On 23 January, Richey was interviewed by the Japanese magazine *Music Life*. It would be his last-known interview.

The guitarist left London's Embassy Hotel at 7 a.m. on the morning of 1 February 1995. He visited his home in Cardiff, where he left his passport, credit card and Prozac. He drove his Vauxhall Cavalier to Aust motorway services by the Severn Bridge – a notorious spot for suicides – where it was discovered with a flat battery on 17 February. And then, nothing. A number of reported sightings remained unconfirmed. A mountain of macabre newspaper speculation turned up no clues. It was as if Richey had simply disappeared off the face of the earth.

Is Richey dead? Despite the best efforts of the police, family and friends, the mystery surrounding his disappearance remains unsolved. The police file remains open, but inactive, at the National Missing Persons Bureau. After a certain time, the family of a missing person are entitled to have the person declared dead and apply for his estate, but a statement issued by Sony in early 2003 said otherwise: 'For the family of Richey Edwards and the members of the Manic Street Preachers nothing has changed,' and the remaining band members continue to pay royalties into a bank account for him.

THE WHITES' WEDDING

DETROIT, 1996

There was a time when rock 'n' roll stars (particularly male ones) found it useful to keep fairly quiet about being married – or to simply avoid the institution altogether, of course. The stories are legion about how Elvis would deny having a regular girlfriend for years after first dating Priscilla when he was still in the army in Germany. And John Lennon went to great lengths in the early days of Beatlemania to hide the fact that he not only had a wife, Cynthia, but a small son as well.

Getting hitched has become less of an issue in recent years, however, although the latest boy-band heart-throbs probably still have to avoid any mention of wives or girlfriends on their way up the slippery slope of success (that's far easier to slide down than climb up). But, in the more 'mature' world of rock, such marital matters don't seem to be of concern anymore.

Even weirder then, was the case of the quirky 'brother and sister' double act from Detroit, the White Stripes. Looking oddly similar with their jet-black hair and ashen complexions, the dynamic punk/R & B duo of guitarist/vocalist Jack White and drummer Meg White got plenty of mileage out of the fact that they were a brother-and-sister team, the two youngest in a family of ten. It later transpired, after first being exposed in 2001 by a writer on the *Detroit Free Press,* that the two were in fact a once-married couple – their 1996 marriage certificate showing that Jack's real name was John Anthony Gillis. Divorced in March 2000, the sibling scam was put about just in time for their debut in the charts the following year.

255

MR LITE GOES HEAVY

LOS ANGELES, 1997

Some big-name stars are famous for unexpectedly changing gear – Bob Dylan going electric, Ray Charles going country and so on – but a most unlikely style transformation came in 1997, with a bizarre 'comeback' by fifties pop crooner Pat Boone.

Boone came to fame by covering early rock 'n' roll classics and making them even bigger hits as a consequence, starting with Fats Domino's 'Ain't That A Shame' in 1955. He was noted for his whiter-than-white clean-cut image, and was allegedly so particular about grammar that he refused to sing the line as 'Ain't that a shame', preferring his own rendition of 'Isn't that a shame'. Boone's version went to Number One, the first of many hits. Other watered-down covers of rock 'n' roll and R & B songs by Boone included Little Richard's 'Tutti Frutti' and 'Long Tall Sally', and Ivory Joe Hunter's 'I Almost Lost My Mind.' So anodyne did he consider the Boone versions that pioneer DJ, Alan Freed, who promoted black R & B to white audiences, refused to play any Boone records on his radio shows.

Boone's image was definitely squeaky clean, from his sparkling teeth to his trademark white sneakers – a newspaper once described him as 'Elvis without the Pelvis'! So it came as no surprise when he turned to religious evangelism in the seventies, for a time only making gospel records. He also formed the Boone Family Singers with his wife and daughters, and together they recorded several Christian albums.

It came as even more of a shock, therefore, when in 1997 he

256

appeared at the American Music Awards dressed in chains and a leather vest, sporting sunglasses and fake tattoos. He said he had turned to heavy metal after listening to a tape of music by Metallica, Deep Purple and Van Halen. Presenting the award for 'Hard Rock – Heavy Metal', he deadpanned to co-presenter and metal godfather Alice Cooper, 'Alice, they're laughing at you,' to which Cooper replied, 'Does this mean heavy metal is dead?' Boone was also promoting an album of covers of heavy-metal classics set to a big-band sound. Entitled *Pat Boone in Metal Mood: No More Mr Nice Guy*, it was sung in the same anodyne style that had worked for him in the fifties. It went on to be a major seller in the US, but there was the inevitable backlash, which resulted in his Christian television series being cancelled.

IN EXCESS: HOW MICHAEL HUTCHENCE DIED

SYDNEY, AUSTRALIA, 1997

The death of Australian rock singer Michael Hutchence came as one of the biggest shocks in the recent annals of rock 'n' roll, particularly the bizarre circumstances in which he was found. With a leather belt tied round the self-locking device on a door, and the other end round his neck, he was found hanged, naked, in a hotel bedroom. And even though a verdict of suicide was delivered, rumours persisted that Hutchence's death was the result of a sado-masochistic perversion gone hideously wrong after an all-night orgy of sex and drugs.

Michael Hutchence's band INXS were enjoying something of a comeback when he flew into his home town of Sydney on 18 November 1997. After a stunning series of hits in the eighties, INXS had drifted apart somewhat by the mid-nineties, a separation accelerated by the departure of their Svengali-like manager C M Murphy in 1995. It was Murphy who had been the guiding hand behind their success for fifteen years, and when he left, it looked to many that they might be splitting up, especially as front-man Hutchence was working on a solo album.

But now, two years after their manager's departure, they were back, albeit not surrounded by the fan and media fervour that accompanied their every move a decade earlier. The previous year they'd released *Elegantly Wasted* to a muted response in the trend-driven rock press and, as he arrived back on Australian soil, Hutchence had good reason to feel positive about his professional future.

On a personal level, however, things hadn't been quite as straightforward in recent months. Over the previous couple of years he'd found what seemed to be the love of his life in Paula Yates (the British TV presenter who'd previously been married to rock singer turned poverty campaigner Bob Geldof) and Hutchence was now the proud father of a daughter, Tiger Lily. But back in the UK, Yates and Geldof had been engaged in a traumatic legal battle for the custody of the two daughters from their marriage, Peaches and Pixie. Hutchence wanted all three girls to move to Australia with Paula so they could settle as a family, but clearly Bob was having nothing of that.

In the immediate future, he'd planned to bring Paula and the girls over for a three-month holiday, but (understandably) Geldof wouldn't have that either, as it would interfere with his daughters' schooling. The day after Hutchence arrived in Sydney, the two parties' lawyers were arguing the case for and against the holiday plan in the High Court in London. This was just the latest shot in the custody battle that had been raging for months, much to Michael Hutchence's increasing frustration and anger.

Despite his anxiety at having to leave Paula and the girls in London, the singer sounded positive when he briefly chatted to the press on his way out of Sydney's Mascot airport. He told them he was back to rehearse and record a TV show at the ABC studios with INXS, who were looking forward to a thirteen-date Australian tour; he then made for the smart Ritz Carlton Hotel in Double Bat where he checked in under the name of 'Murray River'.

The next day, 19 November, Michael relaxed, made a few phone calls and caught up with a couple of old friends; then, the day after, a Thursday, he had breakfast with his father Kell Hutchence and rehearsed with the band at the Gore Hill studios of the Australian Broadcasting Corporation. That day he was also understood to have had several prescriptions filled, one of which was for Prozac.

Friday, and the band were rehearsing again at the ABC

studios, this time with a film being made of the run-through. In retrospect, one shot of the film was oddly telling; not realising he was on camera, the movie caught Hutchence sitting on a stool looking utterly dejected and strangely troubled.

That evening he met his father again, for dinner at an Indian restaurant. Talking to newspapers after his son's death, Kell Hutchence recalled how Michael had confessed he was depressed about the wrangling over the custody issue, speaking of a 'vendetta' being waged against him and Paula. The father also said in an interview in UK *Hello!* magazine that he felt there was a greater pressure on his son over the upcoming tour than Michael would admit; that, and the Geldof/Yates crisis increased his reliance on 'booze, Prozac and other substances'. When he dropped his son off at the Ritz Carlton at 10.30 that night, it was the last time Kell Hutchence would see him.

What happened next that evening can be pieced together from the accounts of various witnesses questioned by the police and subsequently interviewed in the press. First, there was a somewhat mysterious woman named as 'Karen' who met Hutchence in his room soon after his father dropped him off. She had apparently known the singer for fifteen years, but insisted that she didn't have a sexual relationship with him. She never revealed why she went to his room, or what went on when she was there, but confirmed that he was 'saturated' with the variety of medications he was taking, including Keflex, one of the strongest antibiotics on the market. Also never explained was why this woman would have such an intimate knowledge of the drugs the rock star was taking, coupled with her insistence that there were no hard drugs on the scene.

Hutchence was seen by three women at around 11 p.m. as they shared the hotel elevator, the girls confirming that he looked like he was a 'bit high' on something, but seemed happy enough. From the lift he went to the hotel piano bar, where several witnesses said he was in good spirits. He was joined there by an old friend (and ex-lover) Kym Wilson, who was with her boyfriend. The three went up to Michael's room where, according to Wilson, they talked for six hours, the singer mainly telling his visitors how he was concerned about the outcome of the legal battle with Bob Geldof, and how Paula was supposed to be phoning him that night with the latest news about the case.

By the time the call came through – just to tell him they still hadn't got a judge for the case – it was 4.30 a.m. and way past time for his guests to go home. That, according to Kym Wilson's statement, was the last time anyone saw Michael Hutchence alive – and the rumours began flying round soon after that the three (and possibly four if one counted the mysterious 'Karen') were involved in a wild sex and drugs orgy that got out of hand.

What is for certain is that between about 5 a.m. and 10 a.m., Hutchence made and received over a dozen calls, including one from Paula Yates saying that the custody hearing had been postponed so she couldn't come out with the children right then. After that call, a desperate-sounding Hutchence rang Bob Geldof, begging him to let the children come to Australia. According to Martha Troup, the INXS manager at that time, he must have just snapped in the early hours of that morning.

Increasingly confused-sounding calls were made by Hutchence and received on answering machines, to Troup, an ex-lover Michelle Bennett, and members of the band. Finally a second call to Bennett got through, who was so concerned by the tone of his voice that she rushed to the singer's hotel. After knocking on the door of his room at 10.30 a.m. she left, there being no response. A maid eventually found Michael Hutchence hanging on the inside of that hotel room door. It was 11.55 a.m.

BITTER SWEET HIT

LONDON, 1997

Behind the key track on the Verve's 1997 album *Urban Hymns*, 'Bitter Sweet Symphony', is one of the most convoluted stories of copyright wrangling in rock 'n' roll. Verve vocalist Richard Ashcroft, who wrote the tune, made no secret of the fact that it was based around a sample of a high violin line on a record made in 1966.

Just to be on the safe side copyright-wise, the band's management decided they should come to some arrangement with the holders of the rights to the music from which it was culled, before they released the track as a single. As it happens, the owner of those rights was Allen Klein, the notorious American manager who looked after both the Beatles and the Rolling Stones business in the late sixties. When the Verve single became a huge hit, making the Number Two position in the UK pop chart in June 1997, the Klein camp decided the Brit band had used more of the material than had been agreed to, and took legal action accordingly. The result was that the Verve relinquished 100 per cent of the song's publishing income to Klein's ABKCO organisation.

The sample, however, had actually come from a version of the Rolling Stones' 'The Last Time' by the Andrew Oldham Orchestra on *The Rolling Stones Songbook* – a collection of re-workings of Rolling Stones hits by session musicians. The covers LP had been organised by Oldham (the Stones' ex-manager) and the source of the disputed sample – the high violin part – had originally been created by the session's arranger David Sinclair Whittaker, who was just paid a flat fee for the session.

But, as any Rolling Stones aficionado will tell you, the group's own 1965 hit 'The Last Time' was itself actually adapted from an old number of the same name by the Staples Singers, though credited to Mick Jagger and Keith Richards. 'Bitter Sweet Symphony' on the Verve album is now likewise down as having been written by Jagger and Richards, with lyrics attributed to Richard Ashcroft. Credited as being performed by 'The Andrew Oldham Orchestra', there's no mention of the Staples Singers, David Sinclair Whittaker or indeed the Verve.

A MONSTER RAVING ROCKER

HARROW, MIDDLESEX, 1999

One of rock 'n' roll's true eccentrics, Screamin' Lord Sutch is the only rock star who was better known as the leader of a political party. For a couple of decades of British elections and by-elections, the Monster Raving Loony Party was a regular feature, with David Sutch as its leader and most frequent candidate.

David Edward Sutch was born in Harrow, West London in 1942 and, as a teenager in the fifties, was typically entranced by rock 'n' roll. In 1959 he first put together a group, the Raving Savages, even though he didn't play an instrument and could hardly sing in tune. But rock music was still something of a novelty, and novelty – plus a life-long sense of the absurd – was what Sutch was all about.

Screamin' Lord Sutch and the Savages passed an audition to play at London's 2 i's coffee bar, a launching-pad venue in the latter half of the fifties for every up-and-coming British rocker from Tommy Steele to Cliff Richard. It wasn't long before they had a record out on the Decca label, the quasi-shock-horror 'Jack the Ripper' – and Sutch honed his stage act to suit.

Sutch would come on stage in a coffin wearing Dracula-style make-up and Victorian top hat, wielding a knife dripping fake blood and accompanied by lots of 'Hammer horror' stage effects. The act became a permanent and well-loved feature on the early sixties UK rock scene; they played the Star Club in Hamburg with the Beatles, and the embryo Rolling Stones were keen enough fans to actually recruit Savages Carlo Little, Nicky Hopkins and Rick Brown into their early line-up.

A number of future rock stars would pass through the ranks of Sutch's band, including Jimi Hendrix's bass player Noel Redding, Deep Purple's Richie Blackmore and Procul Harum's Matthew Fisher. Additionally, the Who's future drummer Keith Moon would sit in occasionally with the madcap outfit.

In 1970, Sutch even made an all-star album on prestigious US label Atlantic, *Lord Sutch And Heavy Friends*, with superstar guitarists including Jeff Beck and Jimmy Page. However, by that time, Sutch had become more of a household name in the UK via politics.

His debut foray into electioneering came in 1963 in the wake of the political scandal involving the British Secretary of State for War, John Profumo, call girl Christine Keeler and alleged Russian agents. At a by-election triggered by Profumo's resignation, Sutch put himself up as a candidate for his self-styled National Teenage Party, with a manifesto that included votes at eighteen, a network of commercial radio stations and knighthoods for rock stars – all of which of course eventually happened.

Later in the sixties, Sutch formed the Monster Raving Loony Party and contested every by-election that came up, invariably losing his deposit for not getting the requisite minimum number of votes. In general elections, the party even fought a number of seats, with Sutch's fellow Monster Raving Loony Party members also standing and, like their leader, also inevitably losing their deposits.

Sutch's political policies were as tongue-in-cheek humorous as they were bizarre –skiing trips to the so-called European 'butter mountain', a channel-tunnel link to the tax haven of Jersey, giving large pets the vote, getting rid of January and February so that winters would be shorter, and demoting Prime Minister John Major to Private!

With his trademark leopard-skin suit and top hat festooned with rosettes, he became a familiar figure on British television at election time and, after three decades of heading the

Monster Raving Loony Party, was named in the *Guinness Book of Records* as 'the longest serving political leader'.

Sutch carried on playing rock 'n' roll, and was a regular attraction on the 'rock Revival' circuit, but by the late nineties increasing financial problems took their toll. When his eighty-year-old mother died in the West London home they shared in 1997, it affected Sutch deeply. Also, his political 'career' hit crisis point when the deposit for election candidates was raised from £100 to £1,000. Finally, on 16 June 1999, Screamin' Lord Sutch, one of British rock 'n' roll's great characters, hanged himself in the hallway of his mother's home.

MARILYN MANSON AS WILLIE WONKA

HOLLYWOOD, 2001

Shock-horror rocker Marilyn Manson has attracted a number of myths in his time, mostly one suspects of his own creation. One of the favourites some fans still believe, was that Manson, born Brian Warner, was the nerd-like bespectacled child-actor Josh Saviano, who played Paul Pfeiffer, best friend of Kevin Arnold on hit US TV show *The Wonder Years*, which was broadcast from 1988 to 1993.

At the height of his notoriety in the mid-nineties, Manson also got plenty of mileage out of the rumour that he had had a rib removed so he could perform oral sex on himself! That was just one more tale to titillate Manson fans (of which there were many) and foes (of which there were probably an equal number), along with the suggestion that he'd had breast implants, replaced one eye with a testicle . . . and the list goes on.

But one story that did have a basis in truth was in 2001 when he was offered the part of Willie Wonka in the remake of the 1971 film *Willie Wonka and the Chocolate Factory*. The part in the film – entitled, like Roald Dahl's original book, *Charlie and the Chocolate Factory* – eventually went to Johnny Depp. 'I really see the movie as a metaphor,' Manson said to the *Sun* newspaper at the time of the offer (that for one reason or another never followed through). 'I see Willy Wonka as Satan because he presents people with the temptation of picking good and evil, and they all pick evil.'

267

THE WHO'S TOWNSHEND WARNS
OF DANGERS OF LOUD MUSIC

RICHMOND, SURREY, 2005

In 1976, the Who were named as the world's loudest rock band in the *Guinness Book of World Records*, after a show in England when the volume of their music reached an ear-splitting 120 decibels. There was a touch of irony, therefore, when at the end of 2005 the band's lead guitarist Pete Townshend put out a warning to a new generation of music fans against the dangers of hearing damage incurred by listening to loud music.

Writing on his own website, the 60-year-old veteran rocker, who has suffered ear damage throughout his career, said the problem was particularly relevant to the 'i-pod' generation, as more and more fans listen to their music with the aid of earphones, where he believes the risk is greatest.

Townshend explained how he'd had hearing problems through the seventies and eighties, after years of playing with the Who, but found in 1989 that if he used smaller guitar rigs, he could play a whole tour without his hearing getting any worse. 'A lot of fans complained my sound was not what it used to be, but there was no way I could go back to massive six foot high amplifier rigs.'

The more recent problem he had with his ears, however, was directly related to spending hours in the recording studio, listening to music through earphones for most of the time. He explained that he has to 'rest' his ears for 36 hours at a time to restore his hearing after long studio work. This, Townshend felt, was an ironic 'payback' for having been one of the founders of high-energy, high-volume rock.

'I have unwittingly helped to invent and refine a type of music that makes its principal proponents deaf,' he reflected. 'The rewards are great – money, fame, adulation and a real sense of self-worth and achievement. But music is a calling for life. You can write it when you're deaf, but you can't hear it or perform it.'

He referred to a TV film of the Who playing a concert in August 2000, in which John Entwhistle plays a bass solo which is constantly falling out of time with the drummer; that, explained Townshend, was because the bass player simply couldn't hear properly anymore.

Townshend went on to warn of any prolonged listening that utilises earphones, not just involving people working in recording studios but the growing millions of music fans who access their 'sounds' via portable MP3 players, home computers and, increasingly, mobile phones.

'My intuition tells me there is terrible trouble ahead,' the guitarist continued, proposing that the real downside of downloading music will not be that musicians and writers might get their music 'stolen', but that consumers will radically impair their ability to hear the music in the first place.

So it seemed doubly incongruous that while the sexagenarian guitar basher was warning music fans of the threat that listening to music could pose to their health, he and his seasoned colleagues were also announcing another – presumably ear-splitting – world tour.

And it was even more ironic that the man who addressed 'My Generation' in the Who's anthemic call to youth in 1965 would, forty years on, warn another generation of the dangers of listening to that loud rock 'n' roll music.